ISEE MIDDLE LEVEL MATH FOR BEGINNERS

The Ultimate Step by Step Guide to Preparing for the ISEE Middle Level Math Test

By

Reza Nazari

About Effortless Math Education

Effortless Math Education operates the www.effortlessmath.com website, which prepares and publishes Test prep and Mathematics learning resources. Effortless Math authors' team strives to prepare and publish the best quality Mathematics learning resources to make learning Math easier for all. We Help Students Learn to Love Mathematics.

All inquiries should be addressed to:
info@effortlessMath.com
www.EffortlessMath.com

ISBN: 978-1-63719-215-3

Published by: **Effortless Math Education Inc**

for Online Math Practice Visit www.EffortlessMath.com

Welcome to
ISEE Middle Level Math Prep 2022

Thank you for choosing Effortless Math for your ISEE Middle Level Math test preparation and congratulations on making the decision to take the ISEE Middle Level test! It's a remarkable move you are taking, one that shouldn't be diminished in any capacity. That's why you need to use every tool possible to ensure you succeed on the test with the highest possible score, and this extensive study guide is one such tool.

If math has never been a strong subject for you, **don't worry**! This book will help you prepare for (and even ACE) the ISEE Middle Level test's math section. As test day draws nearer, effective preparation becomes increasingly more important. Thankfully, you have this comprehensive study guide to help you get ready for the test. With this guide, you can feel confident that you will be more than ready for the ISEE Middle Level Math test when the time comes.

First and foremost, it is important to note that this book is a study guide and not a textbook. It is best read from cover to cover. Every lesson of this "self-guided math book" was carefully developed to ensure that you are making the most effective use of your time while preparing for the test. This up-to-date guide reflects the 2022 test guidelines and will put you on the right track to hone your math skills, overcome exam anxiety, and boost your confidence, so that you can have your best to succeed on the ISEE Middle Level Math test.

This study guide will:

☑ Explain the format of the ISEE Middle Level Math test.

☑ Describe specific test-taking strategies that you can use on the test.

☑ Provide ISEE Middle Level Math test-taking tips.

☑ Review all ISEE Middle Level Math concepts and topics you will be tested on.

☑ Help you identify the areas in which you need to concentrate your study time.

☑ Offer exercises that help you develop the basic math skills you will learn in each section.

☑ Give **2 realistic and full-length practice tests** (featuring new question types) with detailed answers to help you measure your exam readiness and build confidence.

This resource contains everything you will ever need to succeed on the ISEE Middle Level Math test. You'll get in-depth instructions on every math topic as well as tips and techniques on how to answer each question type. You'll also get plenty of practice questions to boost your test-taking confidence.

In addition, in the following pages you'll find:

➢ **How to Use This Book Effectively** – This section provides you with step-by-step instructions on how to get the most out of this comprehensive study guide.

➢ **How to study for the ISEE Middle Level Math Test** – A six-step study program has been developed to help you make the best use of this book and prepare for your ISEE

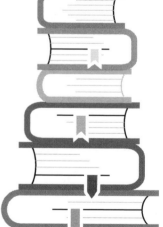

Middle Level Math test. Here you'll find tips and strategies to guide your study program and help you understand ISEE Middle Level Math and how to ace the test.

➢ **ISEE Middle Level Math Review** – Learn everything you need to know about the ISEE Middle Level Math test.

➢ **ISEE Middle Level Math Test-Taking Strategies** – Learn how to effectively put these recommended test-taking techniques into use for improving your ISEE Middle Level Math score.

➢ **Test Day Tips** – Review these tips to make sure you will do your best when the big day comes.

Effortless Math's ISEE Middle Level Online Center

Effortless Math Online ISEE Middle Level Center offers a complete study program, including the following:

✓ Step-by-step instructions on how to prepare for the ISEE Math test

✓ Numerous ISEE Math worksheets to help you measure your math skills

✓ Complete list of ISEE Math formulas

✓ Video lessons for all ISEE Math topics

✓ Full-length ISEE Math practice tests

✓ And much more...

No Registration Required.

Visit effortlessmath.com/ISEEMiddle to find your online ISEE Middle Level Math resources.

How to Use This Book Effectively

Look no further when you need a study guide to improve your math skills to succeed on the math portion of the ISEE Middle Level test. Each chapter of this comprehensive guide to the ISEE Middle Level Math will provide you with the knowledge, tools, and understanding needed for every topic covered on the test.

It's imperative that you understand each topic before moving onto another one, as that's the way to guarantee your success. Each topic provides you with examples and a step-by-step guide of every concept to better understand the content that will be on the test. To get the best possible results from this book:

➢ **Begin studying long before your test date**. This provides you ample time to learn the different math concepts. The earlier you begin studying for the test, the sharper your skills will be. Do not procrastinate! Provide yourself with plenty of time to learn the concepts and feel comfortable that you understand them when your test date arrives.

➢ **Practice consistently**. Study ISEE Middle Level Math concepts at least 20 to 30 minutes a day. Remember, slow and steady wins the race, which can be applied to preparing for the ISEE Middle Level Math test. Instead of cramming to tackle everything at once, be patient and learn the math topics in short bursts.

➢ Whenever you get a math problem wrong, **mark it off, and review it later** to make sure you understand the concept.

➢ Start each session by **looking over the previous material.**

➢ Once you've reviewed the book's lessons, **take the practice test at the back of the book** to gauge your level of readiness. Then, review your results. Read detailed answers and solutions for each question you missed.

➢ **Take another practice test** to get an idea of how ready you are to take the actual exam. Taking the practice tests will give you the confidence you need on test day. Simulate the ISEE Middle Level testing environment by sitting in a quiet room free from distraction. Make sure to clock yourself with a timer.

How to Study for the ISEE Middle Level Math Test

Studying for the ISEE Middle Level Math test can be a really daunting and boring task. What's the best way to go about it? Is there a certain study method that works better than others? Well, studying for the ISEE Middle Level Math can be done effectively. The following six-step program has been designed to make preparing for the ISEE Middle Level Math test more efficient and less overwhelming.

Step 1 - Create a study plan
Step 2 - Choose your study resources
Step 3 - Review, Learn, Practice
Step 4 - Learn and practice test-taking strategies
Step 5 - Learn the ISEE Middle Level Test format and take practice tests
Step 6 - Analyze your performance

STEP 1: Create a Study Plan

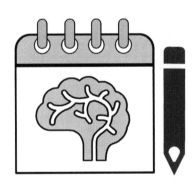

It's always easier to get things done when you have a plan. Creating a study plan for the ISEE Middle Level Math test can help you to stay on track with your studies. It's important to sit down and prepare a study plan with what works with your life, school, and any other obligations you may have. Devote enough time each day to studying. It's also a great idea to break down each section of the exam into blocks and study one concept at a time.

It's important to understand that there is no "right" way to create a study plan. Your study plan will be personalized based on your specific needs and learning style.

Follow these guidelines to create an effective study plan for your ISEE Middle Level Math test:

★ **Analyze your learning style and study habits** – Everyone has a different learning style. It is essential to embrace your individuality and the unique way you learn. Think about what works and what doesn't work for you. Do you prefer ISEE Middle Level Math prep books or a combination of textbooks and video lessons? Does it work better for you if you study every night for thirty minutes or is it more effective to study in the morning before going to school?

★ **Evaluate your schedule** – Review your current schedule and find out how much time you can consistently devote to ISEE Math study.

★ **Develop a schedule** – Now it's time to add your study schedule to your calendar like any other obligation. Schedule time for study, practice, and review. Plan out which topic you will study on which day to ensure that you're devoting enough time to each concept. Develop a study plan that is mindful, realistic, and flexible.

★ **Stick to your schedule** – A study plan is only effective when it is followed consistently. You should try to develop a study plan that you can follow for the length of your study program.

★ **Evaluate your study plan and adjust as needed** – Sometimes you need to adjust your plan when you have new commitments. Check in with yourself regularly to make sure that you're not falling behind in your study plan. Remember, the most important thing is sticking to your plan. Your study plan is all about helping you be more productive. If you find that your study plan is not as effective as you want, don't get discouraged. It's okay to make changes as you figure out what works best for you.

STEP 2: Choose Your Study Resources

There are numerous textbooks and online resources available for the ISEE Middle Level Math test, and it may not be clear where to begin. Don't worry! This study guide provides everything you need to fully prepare for your ISEE Middle Level Math test. In addition to the book content, you can also use Effortless Math's online resources. (video lessons, worksheets, formulas, etc.) On each page, there is a  link (and a QR code) to an online webpage which provides a comprehensive review of the topic, step-by-step instruction, video tutorial, and numerous examples and exercises to help you fully understand the concept.

You can also visit EffortlessMath.com/ISEEMiddle to find your online ISEE Middle Level Math resources.

STEP 3: Review, Learn, Practice

This ISEE Middle Level Math study guide breaks down each subject into specific skills or content areas. For instance, the percent concept is separated into different topics–percent calculation, percent increase and decrease, percent problems, etc. Use this study guide and Effortless Math online ISEE Middle Level center to help you go over all key math concepts and topics on the ISEE Middle Level Math test.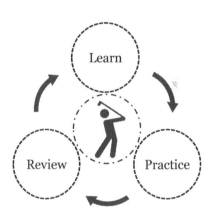

As you read each topic, take notes or highlight the concepts you would like to go over again in the future. If you're unfamiliar with a topic or something is difficult for you, use the link (or the QR code) at the bottom of the page to find the webpage that provides more instruction about that topic. For each math topic, plenty of instructions, step-by-step guides, and examples are provided to ensure you get a good grasp of the material.

Quickly review the topics you do understand to get a brush-up of the material. Be sure to do the practice questions provided at the end of every chapter to measure your understanding of the concepts.

STEP 4: Learn and Practice Test-taking Strategies

In the following sections, you will find important test-taking strategies and tips that can help you earn extra points. You'll learn how to think strategically and when to guess if you don't know the answer to a question. Using ISEE Middle Level Math test-taking strategies and tips can help you raise your score and do well on the test. Apply test taking strategies on the practice tests to help you boost your confidence.

STEP 5: Learn the ISEE Middle Level Test Format and Take Practice Tests

The ISEE Middle Level *Test Review* section provides information about the structure of the ISEE Middle Level test. Read this section to learn more about the ISEE Middle Level test structure, different test sections, the number of questions in each section, and the section time limits. When you have a prior understanding of the test format and different types of ISEE Middle Level Math questions, you'll feel more confident when you take the actual exam.

Once you have read through the instructions and lessons and feel like you are ready to go – take advantage of both of the full-length ISEE Middle Level Math practice tests available in this study guide. Use the practice tests to sharpen your skills and build confidence.

The ISEE Middle Level Math practice tests offered at the end of the book are formatted similarly to the actual ISEE Middle Level Math test. When you take each practice test, try to simulate actual testing conditions. To take the practice tests, sit in a quiet space, time yourself, and work through as many of the questions as time allows. The practice tests are followed by detailed answer explanations to help you find your weak areas, learn from your mistakes, and raise your ISEE Middle Level Math score.

STEP 6: Analyze Your Performance

After taking the practice tests, look over the answer keys and explanations to learn which questions you answered correctly and which you did not. Never be discouraged if you make a few mistakes. See them as a learning opportunity. This will highlight your strengths and weaknesses.

You can use the results to determine if you need additional practice or if you are ready to take the actual ISEE Middle Level Math test.

Looking for more?

Visit effortlessmath.com/ISEEMiddle to find hundreds of ISEE Middle Level Math worksheets, video tutorials, practice tests, ISEE Middle Level Math formulas, and much more.

Or scan this QR code.

No Registration Required.

ISEE Middle Level Test Review

The Independent School Entrance Exam (ISEE) is a standardized test developed by the Educational Records Bureau for its member schools as part of their admission process.

There are currently four Levels of the ISEE:

- ✓ Primary Level (entering Grades 2 - 4)
- ✓ Lower Level (entering Grades 5 and 6)
- ✓ Middle Level (entering Grades 7 and 8)
- ✓ Upper Level (entering Grades 9 - 12)

There are five sections on the ISEE Middle Level Test:

- o Verbal Reasoning
- o Quantitative Reasoning
- o Reading Comprehension
- o Mathematics Achievement
- o and a 30-minute essay

ISEE Middle Level tests use a multiple-choice format and contain two Mathematics sections:

Quantitative Reasoning

There are 37 questions in the Quantitative Reasoning section and students have 35 minutes to answer the questions. This section contains word problems and quantitative comparisons. The word problems require either no calculation or simple calculation. The quantitative comparison items present two quantities,

(A) and (B), and the student needs to select one of the following four answer choices:

(A) The quantity in Column A is greater.

(B) The quantity in Column B is greater.

(C) The two quantities are equal.

(D) The relationship cannot be determined from the information given.

Mathematics Achievement

There are 47 questions in the Mathematics Achievement section and students have 40 minutes to answer the questions. Mathematics Achievement measures students' knowledge of Mathematics requiring one or more steps in calculating the answer.

ISEE Middle Level Math Test-Taking Strategies

Here are some test-taking strategies that you can use to maximize your performance and results on the ISEE Middle Level Math test.

#1: Use This Approach To Answer Every ISEE Middle Level Math Question

- Review the question to identify keywords and important information.

- Translate the keywords into math operations so you can solve the problem.

- Review the answer choices. What are the differences between answer choices?

- Draw or label a diagram if needed.

- Try to find patterns.

- Find the right method to answer the question. Use straightforward math, plug in numbers, or test the answer choices (backsolving).

- Double-check your work.

#2: Use Educated Guessing

This approach is applicable to the problems you understand to some degree but cannot solve using straightforward math. In such cases, try to filter out as many answer choices as possible before picking an answer. In cases where you don't have a clue about what a certain problem entails, don't waste any time trying to eliminate answer choices. Just choose one randomly before moving onto the next question.

As you can ascertain, direct solutions are the most optimal approach. Carefully read through the question, determine what the solution is using the math you have learned before, then coordinate the answer with one of the choices available to you. Are you stumped? Make your best guess, then move on.

Don't leave any fields empty! Even if you're unable to work out a problem, strive to answer it. Take a guess if you have to. You will not lose points by getting an answer wrong, though you may gain a point by getting it correct!

#3 : Ballpark

A ballpark answer is a rough approximation. When we become overwhelmed by calculations and figures, we end up making silly mistakes. A decimal that is moved by one unit can change an answer from right to wrong, regardless of the number of steps that you went through to get it. That's where ballparking can play a big part.

If you think you know what the correct answer may be (even if it's just a ballpark answer), you'll usually have the ability to eliminate a couple of choices. While answer choices are usually based on the average student error and/or values that are closely tied, you will still be able to weed out choices that are way far afield. Try to find answers that aren't in the proverbial ballpark when you're looking for a wrong answer on a multiple-choice question. This is an optimal approach to eliminating answers to a problem.

#4 : Backsolving

All questions on the ISEE Middle Level Math test will be in multiple-choice format. Many test-takers prefer multiple-choice questions, as at least the answer is right there. You'll typically have five answers to pick from. You simply need to figure out which one is correct. Usually, the best way to go about doing so is "backsolving."

As mentioned earlier, direct solutions are the most optimal approach to answering a question. Carefully read through a problem, calculate a solution, then correspond the answer with one of the choices displayed in front of you. If you can't calculate a solution, your next best approach involves "backsolving."

When backsolving a problem, contrast one of your answer options against the problem you are asked, then see which of them is most relevant. More often than not, answer choices are listed in ascending or descending order. In such cases, try out the choices B or C. If it's not correct, you can go either down or up from there.

#5 : Plugging In Numbers

"Plugging in numbers" is a strategy that can be applied to a wide range of different math problems on the ISEE Middle Level Math test. This approach is typically used to simplify a challenging question so that it is more understandable. By using the strategy carefully, you can find the answer without too much trouble.

The concept is fairly straightforward–replace unknown variables in a problem with certain values. When selecting a number, consider the following:

- Choose a number that's basic (just not too basic). Generally, you should avoid choosing 1 (or even 0). A decent choice is 2.

- Try not to choose a number that is displayed in the problem.

- Make sure you keep your numbers different if you need to choose at least two of them.

- More often than not, choosing numbers merely lets you filter out some of your answer choices. As such, don't just go with the first choice that gives you the right answer.

- If several answers seem correct, then you'll need to choose another value and try again. This time, though, you'll just need to check choices that haven't been eliminated yet.

- If your question contains fractions, then a potential right answer may involve either an LCD (least common denominator) or an LCD multiple.

- 100 is the number you should choose when you are dealing with problems involving percentages.

ISEE Middle Level Math – Test Day Tips

After practicing and reviewing all the math concepts you've been taught, and taking some ISEE Middle Level mathematics practice tests, you'll be prepared for test day. Consider the following tips to be extra-ready come test time.

Before Your Test

What to do the night before:

■ **Relax!** One day before your test, study lightly or skip studying altogether. You shouldn't attempt to learn something new, either. There are plenty of reasons why studying the evening before a big test can work against you. Put it this way–a marathoner wouldn't go out for a sprint before the day of a big race. Mental marathoners–such as yourself–should not study for any more than one hour 24 hours before a ISEE Middle Level test. That's because your brain requires some rest to be at its best. The night before your exam, spend some time with family or friends, or read a book.

■ **Avoid bright screens** - You'll have to get some good shuteye the night before your test. Bright screens (such as the ones coming from your laptop, TV, or mobile device) should be avoided altogether. Staring at such a screen will keep your brain up, making it hard to drift asleep at a reasonable hour.

■ **Make sure your dinner is healthy** - The meal that you have for dinner should be nutritious. Be sure to drink plenty of water as well. Load up on your complex carbohydrates, much like a marathon runner would do. Pasta, rice, and potatoes are ideal options here, as are vegetables and protein sources.

■ **Get your bag ready for test day** - The night prior to your test, pack your bag with your stationery, admissions pass, ID, and any other gear that you need. Keep the bag right by your front door.

■ **Make plans to reach the testing site** - Before going to sleep, ensure that you understand precisely how you will arrive at the site of the test. If parking is something you'll have to find first, plan for it. If you're dependent

on public transit, then review the schedule. You should also make sure that the train/bus/subway/streetcar you use will be running. Find out about road closures as well. If a parent or friend is accompanying you, ensure that they understand what steps they have to take as well.

The Day of the Test

■ **Get up reasonably early, but not too early.**

■ **Have breakfast** - Breakfast improves your concentration, memory, and mood. As such, make sure the breakfast that you eat in the morning is healthy. The last thing you want to be is distracted by a grumbling tummy. If it's not your own stomach making those noises, another test taker close to you might be instead. Prevent discomfort or embarrassment by consuming a healthy breakfast. Bring a snack with you if you think you'll need it.

■ **Follow your daily routine** - Do you watch TV each morning while getting ready for the day? Don't break your usual habits on the day of the test. Likewise, if coffee isn't something you drink in the morning, then don't take up the habit hours before your test. Routine consistency lets you concentrate on the main objective–doing the best you can on your test.

■ **Wear layers** - Dress yourself up in comfortable layers. You should be ready for any kind of internal temperature. If it gets too warm during the test, take a layer off.

■ **Get there on time** - The last thing you want to do is get to the test site late. Rather, you should be there 45 minutes prior to the start of the test. Upon your arrival, try not to hang out with anybody who is nervous. Any anxious energy they exhibit shouldn't influence you.

■ **Leave the books at home** - No books should be brought to the test site. If you start developing anxiety before the test, books could encourage you to do some last-minute studying, which will only hinder you. Keep the books far away–better yet, leave them at home.

- **Make your voice heard** - If something is off, speak to a proctor. If medical attention is needed or if you'll require anything, consult the proctor prior to the start of the test. Any doubts you have should be clarified. You should be entering the test site with a state of mind that is completely clear.

- **Have faith in yourself** - When you feel confident, you will be able to perform at your best. When you are waiting for the test to begin, envision yourself receiving an outstanding result. Try to see yourself as someone who knows all the answers, no matter what the questions are. A lot of athletes tend to use this technique—particularly before a big competition. Your expectations will be reflected by your performance.

During your test

- **Be calm and breathe deeply** - You need to relax before the test, and some deep breathing will go a long way to help you do that. Be confident and calm. You got this. Everybody feels a little stressed out just before an evaluation of any kind is set to begin. Learn some effective breathing exercises. Spend a minute meditating before the test starts. Filter out any negative thoughts you have. Exhibit confidence when having such thoughts.

- **Concentrate on the test** - Refrain from comparing yourself to anyone else. You shouldn't be distracted by the people near you or random noise. Concentrate exclusively on the test. If you find yourself irritated by surrounding noises, earplugs can be used to block sounds off close to you. Don't forget—the test is going to last several hours if you're taking more than one subject of the test. Some of that time will be dedicated to brief sections. Concentrate on the specific section you are working on during a particular moment. Do not let your mind wander off to upcoming or previous sections.

- **Skip challenging questions** - Optimize your time when taking the test. Lingering on a single question for too long will work against you. If you don't know what the answer is to a certain question, use your best guess, and mark the question so you can review it later on. There is no need to spend time attempting to solve something you aren't sure about. That time would be better served handling the questions you can actually answer well. You will not be penalized for getting the wrong answer on a test like this.

- **Try to answer each question individually** - Focus only on the question you are working on. Use one of the test-taking strategies to solve the problem. If you aren't able to come up with an answer, don't get frustrated. Simply skip that question, then move onto the next one.

- **Don't forget to breathe!** Whenever you notice your mind wandering, your stress levels boosting, or frustration brewing, take a thirty-second break. Shut your eyes, drop your pencil, breathe deeply, and let your shoulders relax. You will end up being more productive when you allow yourself to relax for a moment.

- **Review your answer**. If you still have time at the end of the test, don't waste it. Go back and check over your answers. It is worth going through the test from start to finish to ensure that you didn't make a sloppy mistake somewhere.

- **Optimize your breaks** - When break time comes, use the restroom, have a snack, and reactivate your energy for the subsequent section. Doing some stretches can help stimulate your blood flow.

After your test

- **Take it easy** - You will need to set some time aside to relax and decompress once the test has concluded. There is no need to stress yourself out about what you could've said, or what you may have done wrong. At this point, there's nothing you can do about it. Your energy and time would be better spent on something that will bring you happiness for the remainder of your day.

- **Redoing the test** - Did you pass the test? Congratulations! Your hard work paid off!

  If you have failed your test, though, don't worry! The test can be retaken. In such cases, you will need to follow the retake policy. You also need to re-register to take the exam again.

Contents

CHAPTER: **Statistics**   **89**

1 Fractions and Mixed Numbers

Math topics that you'll learn in this chapter:

- ☑ Simplifying Fractions
- ☑ Adding and Subtracting Fractions
- ☑ Multiplying and Dividing Fractions
- ☑ Adding Mixed Numbers
- ☑ Subtracting Mixed Numbers
- ☑ Multiplying Mixed Numbers
- ☑ Dividing Mixed Numbers

1

Simplifying Fractions

- A fraction contains two numbers separated by a bar between them. The bottom number, called the denominator, is the total number of equally divided portions in one whole. The top number, called the numerator, is how many portions you have. And the bar represents the operation of division.

- Simplifying a fraction means reducing it to the lowest terms. To simplify a fraction, evenly divide both the top and bottom of the fraction by $2, 3, 5, 7$, etc.

- Continue until you can't go any further.

Examples:

Example 1. Simplify $\frac{18}{30}$

Solution: To simplify $\frac{18}{30}$, find a number that both 18 and 30 are divisible by. Both are divisible by 6. Then: $\frac{18}{30} = \frac{18 \div 6}{30 \div 6} = \frac{3}{5}$

Example 2. Simplify $\frac{48}{80}$

Solution: To simplify $\frac{48}{80}$, find a number that both 48 and 80 are divisible by. Both are divisible by 8 and 16. Then: $\frac{48}{80} = \frac{48 \div 8}{80 \div 8} = \frac{6}{10}$, 6 and 10 are divisible by 2, then: $\frac{6}{10} = \frac{3}{5}$ or $\frac{48}{80} = \frac{48 \div 16}{80 \div 16} = \frac{3}{5}$

Example 3. Simplify $\frac{40}{120}$

Solution: To simplify $\frac{40}{120}$, find a number that both 40 and 120 are divisible by. Both are divisible by 40, then: $\frac{40}{120} = \frac{40 \div 40}{120 \div 40} = \frac{1}{3}$

Adding and Subtracting Fractions

- For "like" fractions (fractions with the same denominator), add or subtract the numerators (top numbers) and write the answer over the common denominator (bottom numbers).

- Adding and Subtracting fractions with the same denominator:

- $\dfrac{a}{b} + \dfrac{c}{b} = \dfrac{a+c}{b}$ $\dfrac{a}{b} - \dfrac{c}{b} = \dfrac{a-c}{b}$

- Find equivalent fractions with the same denominator before you can add or subtract fractions with different denominators.

- Adding and Subtracting fractions with different denominators:

$$\dfrac{a}{b} + \dfrac{c}{d} = \dfrac{ad+bc}{bd} \qquad \dfrac{a}{b} - \dfrac{c}{d} = \dfrac{ad-bc}{bd}$$

Examples:

Example 4. Find the sum. $\dfrac{2}{3} + \dfrac{1}{2} =$

Solution: These two fractions are "unlike" fractions. (they have different denominators). Use this formula: $\dfrac{a}{b} + \dfrac{c}{d} = \dfrac{ad+cb}{bd}$

Then: $\dfrac{2}{3} + \dfrac{1}{2} = \dfrac{(2)(2)+(3)(1)}{3 \times 2} = \dfrac{4+3}{6} = \dfrac{7}{6}$

Example 5. Find the difference. $\dfrac{3}{5} - \dfrac{2}{7} =$

Solution: For "unlike" fractions, find equivalent fractions with the same denominator before you can add or subtract fractions with different denominators. Use this formula:

$\dfrac{a}{b} - \dfrac{c}{d} = \dfrac{ad-bc}{bd}$

$\dfrac{3}{5} - \dfrac{2}{7} = \dfrac{(3)(7)-(2)(5)}{5 \times 7} = \dfrac{21-10}{35} = \dfrac{11}{35}$

Find more at bit.ly/3x5jfwe

Multiplying and Dividing Fractions

- Multiplying fractions: multiply the top numbers and multiply the bottom numbers. Simplify if necessary. $\frac{a}{b} \times \frac{c}{d} = \frac{a \times c}{b \times d}$

- Dividing fractions: Keep, Change, Flip

- Keep the first fraction, change the division sign to multiplication, and flip the numerator and denominator of the second fraction. Then, solve!

$$\frac{a}{b} \div \frac{c}{d} = \frac{a}{b} \times \frac{d}{c} = \frac{a \times d}{b \times c}$$

Examples:

Example 1. Multiply. $\frac{2}{3} \times \frac{3}{5} =$

Solution: Multiply the top numbers and multiply the bottom numbers.
$\frac{2}{3} \times \frac{3}{5} = \frac{2 \times 3}{3 \times 5} = \frac{6}{15}$

Example 2. Solve. $\frac{3}{4} \div \frac{2}{5} =$

Solution: Keep the first fraction, change the division sign to multiplication, and flip the numerator and denominator of the second fraction.
Then: $\frac{3}{4} \div \frac{2}{5} = \frac{3}{4} \times \frac{5}{2} = \frac{3 \times 5}{4 \times 2} = \frac{15}{8}$

Example 3. Calculate. $\frac{4}{5} \times \frac{3}{4} =$

Solution: Multiply the top numbers and multiply the bottom numbers.
$\frac{4}{5} \times \frac{3}{4} = \frac{4 \times 3}{5 \times 4} = \frac{12}{20}$, simplify: $\frac{12}{20} = \frac{12 \div 4}{20 \div 4} = \frac{3}{5}$

Example 4. Solve. $\frac{5}{6} \div \frac{3}{7} =$

Solution: Keep the first fraction, change the division sign to multiplication, and flip the numerator and denominator of the second fraction.
Then: $\frac{5}{6} \div \frac{3}{7} = \frac{5}{6} \times \frac{7}{3} = \frac{5 \times 7}{6 \times 3} = \frac{35}{18}$

Adding Mixed Numbers

Use the following steps for adding mixed numbers:

- Add whole numbers of the mixed numbers.

- Add the fractions of the mixed numbers.

- Find the Least Common Denominator (LCD) if necessary.

- Add whole numbers and fractions.

- Write your answer in lowest terms.

Examples:

Example 1. Add mixed numbers. $2\frac{1}{2} + 1\frac{2}{3} =$

Solution: Let's rewriting our equation with parts separated, $2\frac{1}{2} + 1\frac{2}{3} = 2 + \frac{1}{2} + 1 + \frac{2}{3}$. Now, add whole number parts: $2 + 1 = 3$

Add the fraction parts $\frac{1}{2} + \frac{2}{3}$. Rewrite to solve with the equivalent fractions. $\frac{1}{2} + \frac{2}{3} = \frac{3}{6} + \frac{4}{6} = \frac{7}{6}$. The answer is an improper fraction (numerator is bigger than denominator). Convert the improper fraction into a mixed number: $\frac{7}{6} = 1\frac{1}{6}$. Now, combine the whole and fraction parts: $3 + 1\frac{1}{6} = 4\frac{1}{6}$

Example 2. Find the sum. $1\frac{3}{4} + 2\frac{1}{2} =$

Solution: Rewriting our equation with parts separated, $1 + \frac{3}{4} + 2 + \frac{1}{2}$. Add the whole number parts:

$1 + 2 = 3$. Add the fraction parts: $\frac{3}{4} + \frac{1}{2} = \frac{3}{4} + \frac{2}{4} = \frac{5}{4}$

Convert the improper fraction into a mixed number: $\frac{5}{4} = 1\frac{1}{4}$.

Now, combine the whole and fraction parts: $3 + 1\frac{1}{4} = 4\frac{1}{4}$

bit.ly/2M4oABB

Find more at

Subtract Mixed Numbers

Use these steps for subtracting mixed numbers.

- Convert mixed numbers into improper fractions. $a\frac{c}{b} = \frac{ab+c}{b}$

- Find equivalent fractions with the same denominator for unlike fractions. (fractions with different denominators)

- Subtract the second fraction from the first one. $\frac{a}{b} - \frac{c}{d} = \frac{ad-bc}{bd}$

- Write your answer in lowest terms.

- If the answer is an improper fraction, convert it into a mixed number.

Examples:

Example 1. Subtract. $2\frac{1}{3} - 1\frac{1}{2} =$

Solution: Convert mixed numbers into fractions: $2\frac{1}{3} = \frac{2\times3+1}{3} = \frac{7}{3}$ and $1\frac{1}{2} = \frac{1\times2+1}{2} = \frac{3}{2}$

These two fractions are "unlike" fractions. (they have different denominators). Find equivalent fractions with the same denominator. Use this formula: $\frac{a}{b} - \frac{c}{d} = \frac{ad-bc}{bd}$

$\frac{7}{3} - \frac{3}{2} = \frac{(7)(2)-(3)(3)}{3\times2} = \frac{14-9}{6} = \frac{5}{6}$

Example 2. Subtract. $3\frac{4}{7} - 2\frac{3}{4} =$

Solution: Convert mixed numbers into fractions: $3\frac{4}{7} = \frac{3\times7+4}{7} = \frac{25}{7}$ and $2\frac{3}{4} = \frac{2\times4+3}{4} = \frac{11}{4}$

Then: $3\frac{4}{7} - 2\frac{3}{4} = \frac{25}{7} - \frac{11}{4} = \frac{(25)(4)-(11)(7)}{7\times4} = \frac{23}{28}$

Multiplying Mixed Numbers

Use the following steps for multiplying mixed numbers:

- Convert the mixed numbers into fractions. $a\frac{c}{b} = a + \frac{c}{b} = \frac{ab + c}{b}$

- Multiply fractions. $\frac{a}{b} \times \frac{c}{d} = \frac{a \times c}{b \times d}$

- Write your answer in lowest terms.

- If the answer is an improper fraction (numerator is bigger than denominator), convert it into a mixed number.

Examples:

Example 1. Multiply. $4\frac{1}{2} \times 2\frac{2}{5} =$

Solution: Convert mixed numbers into fractions, $4\frac{1}{2} = \frac{4 \times 2 + 1}{2} = \frac{9}{2}$ and

$$2\frac{2}{5} = \frac{2 \times 5 + 2}{5} = \frac{12}{5}$$

Apply the fractions rule for multiplication, $\frac{9}{2} \times \frac{12}{5} = \frac{9 \times 12}{2 \times 5} = \frac{108}{10}$

The answer is an improper fraction. Convert it into a mixed number. $\frac{108}{10} = 10\frac{4}{5}$

Example 2. Multiply. $3\frac{2}{3} \times 2\frac{5}{6} =$

Solution: Converting mixed numbers into fractions, $3\frac{2}{3} \times 2\frac{5}{6} = \frac{11}{3} \times \frac{17}{6}$

Apply the fractions rule for multiplication, $\frac{11}{3} \times \frac{17}{6} = \frac{11 \times 17}{3 \times 6} = \frac{187}{18} = 10\frac{7}{18}$

Example 3. Multiply mixed numbers. $5\frac{1}{4} \times 3\frac{3}{8} =$

Solution: Converting mixed numbers to fractions, $5\frac{1}{4} = \frac{21}{4}$ and $3\frac{3}{8} = \frac{27}{8}$. Multiply

two fractions:

$\frac{21}{4} \times \frac{27}{8} = \frac{21 \times 27}{4 \times 8} = \frac{567}{32} = 17\frac{23}{32}$

bit.ly/3aPy7XJ

Find more at

Dividing Mixed Numbers

Use the following steps for dividing mixed numbers:

- Convert the mixed numbers into fractions. $a\frac{c}{b} = a + \frac{c}{b} = \frac{ab+c}{b}$

- Divide fractions: Keep, Change, Flip: Keep the first fraction, change the division sign to multiplication, and flip the numerator and denominator of the second fraction. Then, solve! $\frac{a}{b} \div \frac{c}{d} = \frac{a}{b} \times \frac{d}{c} = \frac{a \times d}{b \times c}$

- Write your answer in lowest terms.

- If the answer is an improper fraction (numerator is bigger than denominator), convert it into a mixed number.

Examples:

Example 1. Solve. $2\frac{1}{3} \div 1\frac{1}{2}$

Solution: Convert mixed numbers into fractions: $2\frac{1}{3} = \frac{2 \times 3 + 1}{3} = \frac{7}{3}$ and $1\frac{1}{2} = \frac{1 \times 2 + 1}{2} = \frac{3}{2}$
Keep, Change, Flip: $\frac{7}{3} \div \frac{3}{2} = \frac{7}{3} \times \frac{2}{3} = \frac{7 \times 2}{3 \times 3} = \frac{14}{9}$. The answer is an improper fraction.
Convert it into a mixed number: $\frac{14}{9} = 1\frac{5}{9}$

Example 2. Solve. $3\frac{3}{4} \div 2\frac{2}{5}$

Solution: Convert mixed numbers to fractions, then solve:
$3\frac{3}{4} \div 2\frac{2}{5} = \frac{15}{4} \div \frac{12}{5} = \frac{15}{4} \times \frac{5}{12} = \frac{75}{48} = 1\frac{9}{16}$

Example 3. Solve. $2\frac{4}{5} \div 1\frac{2}{3}$

Solution: Converting mixed numbers to fractions: $2\frac{4}{5} \div 1\frac{2}{3} = \frac{14}{5} \div \frac{5}{3}$
Keep, Change, Flip: $\frac{14}{5} \div \frac{5}{3} = \frac{14}{5} \times \frac{3}{5} = \frac{14 \times 3}{5 \times 5} = \frac{42}{25} = 1\frac{17}{25}$

Chapter 1: Practices

✍ Simplify each fraction.

1) $\frac{2}{8} =$

2) $\frac{5}{15} =$

3) $\frac{10}{90} =$

4) $\frac{12}{16} =$

5) $\frac{25}{45} =$

6) $\frac{42}{54} =$

7) $\frac{48}{60} =$

8) $\frac{52}{169} =$

✍ Find the sum or difference.

9) $\frac{3}{10} + \frac{2}{10} =$

10) $\frac{4}{9} - \frac{1}{9} =$

11) $\frac{2}{3} + \frac{6}{15} =$

12) $\frac{17}{24} - \frac{5}{8} =$

13) $\frac{7}{54} - \frac{1}{9} =$

14) $\frac{4}{5} - \frac{1}{6} =$

15) $\frac{6}{7} - \frac{3}{8} =$

16) $\frac{2}{13} + \frac{1}{4} =$

✍ Find the products or quotients.

17) $\frac{2}{9} \div \frac{4}{3} =$

18) $\frac{14}{5} \div \frac{28}{35} =$

19) $\frac{9}{25} \times \frac{5}{27} =$

20) $\frac{65}{72} \times \frac{12}{15} =$

✍ Find the sum.

21) $2\frac{1}{5} + 1\frac{2}{5} =$

22) $5\frac{1}{9} + 2\frac{7}{9} =$

23) $2\frac{3}{4} + 1\frac{1}{8} =$

24) $2\frac{2}{7} + 4\frac{1}{21} =$

25) $5\frac{3}{5} + 1\frac{4}{9} =$

26) $3\frac{3}{11} + 4\frac{6}{7} =$

Effortless
Math
Education

✍ Find the difference.

27) $5\frac{1}{3} - 4\frac{2}{3} =$

28) $4\frac{7}{10} - 1\frac{3}{10} =$

29) $3\frac{1}{3} - 2\frac{2}{9} =$

30) $6\frac{1}{2} - 3\frac{1}{3} =$

31) $4\frac{3}{4} - 2\frac{1}{28} =$

32) $4\frac{2}{7} - 3\frac{1}{6} =$

33) $5\frac{3}{10} - 3\frac{3}{4} =$

34) $6\frac{9}{20} - 2\frac{1}{3} =$

✍ Find the products.

35) $1\frac{1}{2} \times 2\frac{3}{7} =$

36) $1\frac{3}{4} \times 1\frac{3}{5} =$

37) $4\frac{1}{2} \times 1\frac{5}{6} =$

38) $1\frac{2}{7} \times 3\frac{1}{5} =$

39) $2\frac{1}{5} \times 5\frac{1}{2} =$

40) $2\frac{1}{2} \times 4\frac{4}{5} =$

41) $3\frac{1}{5} \times 4\frac{1}{2} =$

42) $4\frac{9}{10} \times 4\frac{1}{2} =$

✍ Solve.

43) $1\frac{1}{3} \div 1\frac{2}{3} =$

44) $2\frac{1}{4} \div 1\frac{1}{2} =$

45) $5\frac{1}{3} \div 3\frac{1}{2} =$

46) $3\frac{2}{7} \div 1\frac{1}{8} =$

47) $4\frac{1}{5} \div 2\frac{2}{3} =$

48) $1\frac{2}{3} \div 1\frac{3}{8} =$

49) $4\frac{1}{2} \div 2\frac{2}{3} =$

50) $1\frac{2}{11} \div 1\frac{1}{8} =$

Effortless
Math
Education

Effortless

Math

Education

Chapter 1: Answers

1) $\frac{1}{4}$

2) $\frac{1}{3}$

3) $\frac{1}{9}$

4) $\frac{3}{4}$

5) $\frac{5}{9}$

6) $\frac{7}{9}$

7) $\frac{4}{5}$

8) $\frac{4}{13}$

9) $\frac{1}{2}$

10) $\frac{1}{3}$

11) $\frac{16}{15} = 1\frac{1}{15}$

12) $\frac{1}{12}$

13) $\frac{1}{54}$

14) $\frac{19}{30}$

15) $\frac{27}{56}$

16) $\frac{21}{52}$

17) $\frac{1}{6}$

18) $\frac{7}{2} = 3\frac{1}{2}$

19) $\frac{1}{15}$

20) $\frac{13}{18}$

21) $3\frac{3}{5}$

22) $7\frac{8}{9}$

23) $3\frac{7}{8}$

24) $6\frac{1}{3}$

25) $7\frac{2}{45}$

26) $8\frac{10}{77}$

27) $\frac{2}{3}$

28) $3\frac{2}{5}$

29) $1\frac{1}{9}$

30) $3\frac{1}{6}$

31) $2\frac{5}{7}$

32) $1\frac{5}{42}$

33) $1\frac{11}{20}$

34) $4\frac{7}{60}$

35) $3\frac{9}{14}$

36) $2\frac{4}{5}$

37) $8\frac{1}{4}$

38) $4\frac{4}{35}$

39) $12\frac{1}{10}$

40) 12

41) $14\frac{2}{5}$

42) $22\frac{1}{20}$

43) $\frac{4}{5}$

44) $1\frac{1}{2}$

45) $1\frac{11}{21}$

46) $2\frac{58}{63}$

47) $1\frac{23}{40}$

48) $1\frac{7}{33}$

49) $1\frac{11}{16}$

50) $1\frac{5}{99}$

CHAPTER

2 Decimals

Math topics that you'll learn in this chapter:

- ☑ Comparing Decimals
- ☑ Rounding Decimals
- ☑ Adding and Subtracting Decimals
- ☑ Multiplying and Dividing Decimals

Comparing Decimals

- A decimal is a fraction written in a special form. For example, instead of writing $\frac{1}{2}$ you can write 0.5

- A Decimal Number contains a Decimal Point. It separates the whole number part from the fractional part of a decimal number.

- Let's review decimal place values: Example: 53.9861

5: tens   3: ones   9: tenths

8: hundredths   6: thousandths   1: tens thousandths

- To compare decimals, compare each digit of two decimals in the same place value. Start from left. Compare hundreds, tens, ones, tenth, hundredth, etc.

- To compare numbers, use these symbols:

Equal to =,   Less than <,   Greater than >

Greater than or equal ≥,   Less than or equal ≤

Examples:

Example 1. Compare 0.03 and 0.30.

Solution: 0.30 *is greater than* 0.03, because the tenth place of 0.30 is 3, but the tenth place of 0.03 is zero. Then: 0.03 < 0.30

Example 2. Compare 0.0217 and 0.217.

Solution: 0.217 *is greater than* 0.0217, because the tenth place of 0.217 is 2, but the tenth place of 0.0217 is zero. Then: 0.0217 < 0.217

Rounding Decimals

- We can round decimals to a certain accuracy or number of decimal places. This is used to make calculations easier to do and results easier to understand when exact values are not too important.

- First, you'll need to remember your place values: For example: 12.4869

   1: tens   2: ones   4: tenths

   8: hundredths   6: thousandths   9: tens thousandths

- To round a decimal, first find the place value you'll round to.

- Find the digit to the right of the place value you're rounding to. If it is 5 or bigger, add 1 to the place value you're rounding to and remove all digits on its right side. If the digit to the right of the place value is less than 5, keep the place value and remove all digits on the right.

Examples:

Example 1. Round 4.3679 to the thousandth place value.

Solution: First, look at the next place value to the right, (tens thousandths). It's 9 and it is greater than 5. Thus add 1 to the digit in the thousandth place. The thousandth place is 7. $\rightarrow 7 + 1 = 8$, then,
The answer is 4.368

Example 2. Round 1.5237 to the nearest hundredth.

Solution: First, look at the digit to the right of hundredth (thousandths place value). It's 3 and it is less than 5, thus remove all the digits to the right of hundredth place. Then, the answer is 1.52

Adding and Subtracting Decimals

- Line up the decimal numbers.

- Add zeros to have the same number of digits for both numbers if necessary.

- Remember your place values: For example: 73.5196

    7: tens   3: ones   5: tenths

    1: hundredths   9: thousandths   6: tens thousandths

- Add or subtract using column addition or subtraction.

Examples:

Example 1. Add. $1.7 + 4.12$

Solution: First, line up the numbers: $\begin{array}{r} 1.7 \\ +\,4.12 \\ \hline \end{array}$ → Add a zero to have the same number of digits for both numbers. $\begin{array}{r} 1.70 \\ +\,4.12 \\ \hline \end{array}$ → Start with the hundredths place: $0 + 2 = 2$, $\begin{array}{r} 1.70 \\ +\,4.12 \\ \hline 2 \end{array}$ → Continue with tenths place: $7 + 1 = 8$, $\begin{array}{r} 1.70 \\ +\,4.12 \\ \hline .82 \end{array}$ → Add the ones place: $4 + 1 = 5$, $\begin{array}{r} 1.70 \\ +\,4.12 \\ \hline 5.82 \end{array}$

Example 2. Find the difference. $5.58 - 4.23$

Solution: First, line up the numbers: $\begin{array}{r} 5.58 \\ -\,4.23 \\ \hline \end{array}$ → Start with the hundredths place: $8 - 3 = 5$, $\begin{array}{r} 5.58 \\ -\,4.23 \\ \hline 5 \end{array}$ → Continue with tenths place. $5 - 2 = 3$, $\begin{array}{r} 5.58 \\ -\,4.23 \\ \hline .35 \end{array}$ → Subtract the ones place. $5 - 4 = 1$, $\begin{array}{r} 5.58 \\ -\,4.23 \\ \hline 1.35 \end{array}$

Multiplying and Dividing Decimals

For multiplying decimals:

- Ignore the decimal point and set up and multiply the numbers as you do with whole numbers.

- Count the total number of decimal places in both of the factors.

- Place the decimal point in the product.

For dividing decimals:

- If the divisor is not a whole number, move the decimal point to the right to make it a whole number. Do the same for the dividend.

- Divide similar to whole numbers.

Examples:

Example 1. Find the product. $0.65 \times 0.24 =$

Solution: Set up and multiply the numbers as you do with whole numbers. Line up the numbers: $\begin{array}{r} 65 \\ \times 24 \end{array}$ → Start with the ones place then continue with other digits → $\begin{array}{r} 65 \\ \times 24 \\ \hline 1,560 \end{array}$. Count the total number of decimal places in both of the factors. There are four decimals digits. (two for each factor 0.65 and 0.24) Then: $0.65 \times 0.24 = 0.1560$

Example 2. Find the quotient. $1.20 \div 0.4 =$

Solution: The divisor is not a whole number. Multiply it by 10 to get 4: → $0.4 \times 10 = 4$

Do the same for the dividend to get 12. → $1.20 \times 10 = 12$

Now, divide $12 \div 4 = 3$. The answer is 3.

Chapter 2: Practices

✎ Compare. Use >, =, and <

1) 0.5 ☐ 0.6

2) 0.9 ☐ 0.8

3) 0.1 ☐ 0.2

4) 0.02 ☐ 0.06

5) 0.05 ☐ 0.08

6) 0.12 ☐ 0.09

7) 3.2 ☐ 2.5

8) 4.8 ☐ 8.4

9) 0.005 ☐ 0.05

10) 2.02 ☐ 20.020

11) 55.100 ☐ 55.10

12) 0.44 ☐ 0.440

13) 6.01 ☐ 6.0100

14) 0.77 ☐ 77.0

✎ Round each decimal to the nearest whole number.

15) 5.8

16) 6.4

17) 12.3

18) 9.2

19) 7.6

20) 22.4

21) 6.8

22) 15.9

23) 13.41

24) 16.78

25) 67.58

26) 42.67

27) 55.89

28) 14.32

29) 78.88

30) 98.29

Effortless
Math
Education

✎ **Find the sum or difference.**

31) $12.1 + 36.2 =$ 39) $96.23 - 28.32 =$

32) $56.3 - 22.2 =$ 40) $57.33 + 67.46 =$

33) $45.1 + 12.8 =$ 41) $46.26 - 39.49 =$

34) $27.9 - 16.4 =$ 42) $44.95 + 76.53 =$

35) $98.8 - 56.6 =$ 43) $79.37 - 52.89 =$

36) $28.45 + 13.22 =$ 44) $19.99 + 28.7 =$

37) $16.78 + 45.11 =$ 45) $83.48 - 49.3 =$

38) $86.16 - 72.12 =$ 46) $19.6 + 42.98 =$

✎ **Find the product or quotient.**

47) $3.3 \times 0.2 =$ 55) $2.1 \times 8.4 =$

48) $2.4 \div 0.3 =$ 56) $1.6 \times 4.5 =$

49) $8.1 \times 1.4 =$ 57) $9.2 \times 3.1 =$

50) $4.8 \div 0.2 =$ 58) $36.6 \div 1.6 =$

51) $4.1 \times 0.3 =$ 59) $1.91 \times 5.2 =$

52) $8.6 \div 0.2 =$ 60) $3.65 \times 1.4 =$

53) $9.9 \times 0.8 =$ 61) $24.82 \div 0.4 =$

54) $1.84 \div 0.2 =$ 62) $12.4 \times 4.20 =$

**Effortless
Math
Education**

Chapter 2: Answers

1)	<	22)	16	43)	26.48
2)	>	23)	13	44)	48.69
3)	<	24)	17	45)	34.18
4)	<	25)	68	46)	62.58
5)	<	26)	43	47)	0.66
6)	>	27)	56	48)	8
7)	>	28)	14	49)	11.34
8)	<	29)	79	50)	24
9)	<	30)	98	51)	1.23
10)	<	31)	48.3	52)	43
11)	=	32)	34.1	53)	7.92
12)	=	33)	57.9	54)	9.2
13)	=	34)	11.5	55)	17.64
14)	<	35)	42.2	56)	7.2
15)	6	36)	41.67	57)	28.52
16)	6	37)	61.89	58)	22.875
17)	12	38)	14.04	59)	9.932
18)	9	39)	67.91	60)	5.11
19)	8	40)	124.79	61)	62.05
20)	22	41)	6.77	62)	52.08
21)	7	42)	121.48		

Effortless
Math
Education

3 Integers and Order of Operations

Math topics that you'll learn in this chapter:

- ☑ Adding and Subtracting Integers
- ☑ Multiplying and Dividing Integers
- ☑ Order of Operations
- ☑ Integers and Absolute Value

Adding and Subtracting Integers

- Integers include zero, counting numbers, and the negative of the counting numbers. $\{\dots, -3, -2, -1, 0, 1, 2, 3, \dots\}$

- Add a positive integer by moving to the right on the number line. (you will get a bigger number)

- Add a negative integer by moving to the left on the number line. (you will get a smaller number)

- Subtract an integer by adding its opposite.

Examples:

Example 1. Solve. $(-2) - (-8) =$

Solution: Keep the first number and convert the sign of the second number to its opposite. (change subtraction into addition. Then: $(-2) + 8 = 6$

Example 2. Solve. $4 + (5 - 10) =$

Solution: First, subtract the numbers in brackets, $5 - 10 = -5$.
Then: $4 + (-5) = \rightarrow$ change addition into subtraction: $4 - 5 = -1$

Example 3. Solve. $(9 - 14) + 15 =$

Solution: First, subtract the numbers in brackets, $9 - 14 = -5$
Then: $-5 + 15 = \rightarrow -5 + 15 = 10$

Example 4. Solve. $12 + (-3 - 10) =$

Solution: First, subtract the numbers in brackets, $-3 - 10 = -13$
Then: $12 + (-13) = \rightarrow$ change addition into subtraction: $12 - 13 = -1$

Multiplying and Dividing Integers

Use the following rules for multiplying and dividing integers:

- (negative) × (negative) = positive

- (negative) ÷ (negative) = positive

- (negative) × (positive) = negative

- (negative) ÷ (positive) = negative

- (positive) × (positive) = positive

- (positive) ÷ (negative) = negative

Examples:

Example 1. Solve. $3 \times (-4) =$

Solution: Use this rule: (positive) × (negative) = negative.
Then: $(3) \times (-4) = -12$

Example 2. Solve. $(-3) + (-24 \div 3) =$

Solution: First, divide -24 by 3, the numbers in brackets, use this rule:
(negative) ÷ (positive) = negative. Then: $-24 \div 3 = -8$
$(-3) + (-24 \div 3) = (-3) + (-8) = -3 - 8 = -11$

Example 3. Solve. $(12 - 15) \times (-2) =$

Solution: First, subtract the numbers in brackets,
$12 - 15 = -3 \rightarrow (-3) \times (-2) =$
Now use this rule: (negative) × (negative) = positive $\rightarrow (-3) \times (-2) = 6$

Example 4. Solve. $(12 - 8) \div (-4) =$

Solution: First, subtract the numbers in brackets,
$12 - 8 = 4 \rightarrow (4) \div (-4) =$
Now use this rule: (positive) ÷ (negative) = negative $\rightarrow (4) \div (-4) =$
-1

bit.ly/3pjQW98

Find more at

Order of Operations

- In Mathematics, "operations" are addition, subtraction, multiplication, division, exponentiation (written as b^n), and grouping.

- When there is more than one math operation in an expression, use PEMDAS: (to memorize this rule, remember the phrase "Please Excuse My Dear Aunt Sally".)

  ❖ Parentheses
  ❖ Exponents
  ❖ Multiplication and Division (from left to right)
  ❖ Addition and Subtraction (from left to right)

Examples:

Example 1. Calculate. $(2 + 6) \div (2^2 \div 4) =$

Solution: First, simplify inside parentheses:
$(8) \div (4 \div 4) = (8) \div (1)$, Then: $(8) \div (1) = 8$

Example 2. Solve. $(6 \times 5) - (14 - 5) =$

Solution: First, calculate within parentheses: $(6 \times 5) - (14 - 5) = (30) - (9)$, Then: $(30) - (9) = 21$

Example 3. Calculate. $-4[(3 \times 6) \div (3^2 \times 2)] =$

Solution: First, calculate within parentheses:
$-4[(18) \div (9 \times 2)] = -4[(18) \div (18)] = -4[1]$
multiply -4 and 1. Then: $-4[1] = -4$

Example 4. Solve. $(28 \div 7) + (-19 + 3) =$

Solution: First, calculate within parentheses:
$(28 \div 7) + (-19 + 3) = (4) + (-16)$ Then: $(4) - (16) = -12$

Integers and Absolute Value

- The absolute value of a number is its distance from zero, in either direction, on the number line. For example, the distance of 9 and -9 from zero on number line is 9.

- The absolute value of an integer is the numerical value without its sign. (negative or positive)

- The vertical bar is used for absolute value as in $|x|$.

- The absolute value of a number is never negative; because it only shows, "how far the number is from zero".

Examples:

Example 1. Calculate. $|14 - 2| \times 5 =$

Solution: First, solve $|14 - 2|$, $\rightarrow |14 - 2| = |12|$, the absolute value of 12 is 12, $|12| = 12$ Then: $12 \times 5 = 60$

Example 2. Solve. $\frac{|-24|}{4} \times |5 - 7| =$

Solution: First, find $|-24|$, $\rightarrow$ the absolute value of -24 is 24,
Then: $|-24| = 24$, $\frac{24}{4} \times |5 - 7| =$

Now, calculate $|5 - 7|$, $\rightarrow |5 - 7| = |-2|$, the absolute value of -2 is 2. $|-2| = 2$
then: $\frac{24}{4} \times 2 = 6 \times 2 = 12$

Example 3. Solve. $|8 - 2| \times \frac{|-4 \times 7|}{2} =$

Solution: First, calculate $|8 - 2|$, $\rightarrow |8 - 2| = |6|$, the absolute value of 6 is 6, $|6| = 6$. Then: $6 \times \frac{|-4 \times 7|}{2}$

Now calculate $|-4 \times 7|$, $\rightarrow -4 \times 7 = |-28|$, the absolute value of -28 is 28, $|-28| = 28$ Then: $6 \times \frac{28}{2} = 6 \times 14 = 84$

bit.ly/3aD521u

Find more at

Chapter 3: Practices

✍ Find each sum or difference.

1) $-9 + 16 =$

2) $-18 - 6 =$

3) $-24 + 10 =$

4) $30 + (-5) =$

5) $15 + (-3) =$

6) $(-13) + (-4) =$

7) $25 + (3 - 10) =$

8) $12 - (-6 + 9) =$

9) $5 - (-2 + 7) =$

10) $(-11) + (-5 + 6) =$

11) $(-3) + (9 - 16) =$

12) $(-8) - (13 + 4) =$

13) $(-7 + 9) - 39 =$

14) $(-30 + 6) - 14 =$

15) $(-5 + 9) + (-3 + 7) =$

16) $(8 - 19) - (-4 + 12) =$

17) $(-9 + 2) - (6 - 7) =$

18) $(-12 - 5) - (-4 - 14) =$

✍ Solve.

19) $3 \times (-6) =$

20) $(-32) \div 4 =$

21) $(-5) \times 4 =$

22) $(25) \div (-5) =$

23) $(-72) \div 8 =$

24) $(-2) \times (-6) \times 5 =$

25) $(-2) \times 3 \times (-7) =$

26) $(-1) \times (-3) \times (-5) =$

27) $(-2) \times (-3) \times (-6) =$

28) $(-12 + 3) \times (-5) =$

29) $(-3 + 4) \times (-11) =$

30) $(-9) \times (6 - 5) =$

31) $(-3 - 7) \times (-6) =$

32) $(-7 + 3) \times (-9 + 6) =$

33) $(-15) \div (-17 + 12) =$

34) $(-3 - 2) \times (-9 + 7) =$

35) $(-15 + 31) \div (-2) =$

36) $(-64) \div (-16 + 8) =$

Effortless
Math
Education

✍ Evaluate each expression.

37) $3 + (2 \times 5) =$

38) $(5 \times 4) - 7 =$

39) $(-9 \times 2) + 6 =$

40) $(7 \times 3) - (-5) =$

41) $(-8) + (2 \times 7) =$

42) $(9 - 6) + (3 \times 4) =$

43) $(-19 + 5) + (6 \times 2) =$

44) $(32 \div 4) + (1 - 13) =$

45) $(-36 \div 6) - (12 + 3) =$

46) $(-16 + 5) - (54 \div 9) =$

47) $(-20 + 4) - (35 \div 5) =$

48) $(42 \div 7) + (2 \times 3) =$

49) $(28 \div 4) + (2 \times 6) =$

50) $2[(3 \times 3) - (4 \times 5)] =$

51) $3[(2 \times 8) + (4 \times 3)] =$

52) $2[(9 \times 3) - (6 \times 4)] =$

53) $4[(4 \times 8) \div (4 \times 4)] =$

54) $-5[(10 \times 8) \div (5 \times 8)] =$

✍ Find the answers.

55) $|-5| + |7 - 10| =$

56) $|-4 + 6| + |-2| =$

57) $|-9| + |1 - 9| =$

58) $|-7| - |8 - 12| =$

59) $|9 - 11| + |8 - 15| =$

60) $|-7 + 10| - |-8 + 3| =$

61) $|-12 + 6| - |3 - 9| =$

62) $5 + |2 - 6| + |3 - 4| =$

63) $-4 + |2 - 6| + |1 - 9| =$

64) $|-6| \times |-7| + |2 - 8| =$

65) $|-12| \times |-3| + |4 - 28| =$

66) $|4 \times (-2)| \times |-9| =$

67) $|-3 \times 2| \times |-5| =$

68) $|3 - 12| - |-3 \times 7| =$

69) $|-9| + |-7 \times 5| =$

70) $|-11| + |-6 \times 4| =$

71) $|-4 \times 2 + 6| \times |-2 \times 8| =$

72) $|-1 \times 5 + 2| \times |-4| =$

Effortless Math Education

Chapter 3: Answers

1) 7
2) −24
3) −14
4) 25
5) 12
6) −17
7) 18
8) 9
9) 0
10) −10
11) −10
12) −25
13) −37
14) −38
15) 8
16) −19
17) −6
18) 1
19) −18
20) −8
21) −20
22) −5
23) −9
24) 60

25) 42
26) −15
27) −36
28) 45
29) −11
30) −9
31) 60
32) 12
33) 3
34) 10
35) −8
36) 8
37) 13
38) 13
39) −12
40) 26
41) 6
42) 15
43) −2
44) −4
45) −21
46) −17
47) −23
48) 12

49) 19
50) −22
51) 84
52) 6
53) 8
54) −10
55) 8
56) 4
57) 17
58) 3
59) 9
60) −2
61) 0
62) 10
63) 8
64) 48
65) 60
66) 72
67) 30
68) −12
69) 44
70) 35
71) 32
72) 12

CHAPTER

4 Ratios and Proportions

Math topics that you'll learn in this chapter:

☑ Simplifying Ratios

☑ Proportional Ratios

☑ Similarity and Ratios

Simplifying Ratios

- Ratios are used to make comparisons between two numbers.

- Ratios can be written as a fraction, using the word "to", or with a colon. Example: $\frac{3}{4}$ or "3 to 4" or 3:4

- You can calculate equivalent ratios by multiplying or dividing both sides of the ratio by the same number.

Examples:

Example 1. Simplify. $8:2 =$

Solution: Both numbers 8 and 2 are divisible by 2 , $\Rightarrow 8 \div 2 = 4$, $4 \div 2 = 2$, Then: $8:2 = 4:1$

Example 2. Simplify. $\frac{9}{33} =$

Solution: Both numbers 9 and 33 are divisible by 3, $\Rightarrow$ $33 \div 3 = 11$, $9 \div 3 = 3$, Then: $\frac{9}{33} = \frac{3}{11}$

Example 3. There are 24 students in a class and 10 are girls. Write the ratio of girls to boys.

Solution: Subtract 10 from 24 to find the number of boys in the class. $24 - 10 = 14$. There are 14 boys in the class. So, the ratio of girls to boys is $10:14$. Now, simplify this ratio. Both 14 and 10 are divisible by 2. Then: $14 \div 2 = 7$, and $10 \div 2 = 5$. In the simplest form, this ratio is $5:7$

Example 4. A recipe calls for butter and sugar in the ratio $3:4$. If you're using 9 cups of butter, how many cups of sugar should you use?

Solution: Since you use 9 cups of butter, or 3 times as much, you need to multiply the amount of sugar by 3. Then: $4 \times 3 = 12$. So, you need to use 12 cups of sugar. You can solve this using equivalent fractions: $\frac{3}{4} = \frac{9}{12}$

Proportional Ratios

- Two ratios are proportional if they represent the same relationship.

- A proportion means that two ratios are equal. It can be written in two ways: $\frac{a}{b} = \frac{c}{d}$ $a : b = c : d$

- The proportion $\frac{a}{b} = \frac{c}{d}$ can be written as: $a \times d = c \times b$

Examples:

Example 1. Solve this proportion for x. $\frac{2}{5} = \frac{6}{x}$

Solution: Use cross multiplication: $\frac{2}{5} = \frac{6}{x} \Rightarrow 2 \times x = 6 \times 5 \Rightarrow 2x = 30$

Divide both sides by 2 to find x: $x = \frac{30}{2} \Rightarrow x = 15$

Example 2. If a box contains red and blue balls in ratio of $3 : 5$ red to blue, how many red balls are there if 45 blue balls are in the box?

Solution: Write a proportion and solve. $\frac{3}{5} = \frac{x}{45}$

Use cross multiplication: $3 \times 45 = 5 \times x \Rightarrow 135 = 5x$

Divide to find x: $x = \frac{135}{5} \Rightarrow x = 27$. There are 27 red balls in the box.

Example 3. Solve this proportion for x. $\frac{4}{9} = \frac{16}{x}$

Solution: Use cross multiplication: $\frac{4}{9} = \frac{16}{x} \Rightarrow 4 \times x = 9 \times 16 \Rightarrow 4x = 144$

Divide to find x: $x = \frac{144}{4} \Rightarrow x = 36$

Example 4. Solve this proportion for x. $\frac{5}{7} = \frac{20}{x}$

Solution: Use cross multiplication: $\frac{5}{7} = \frac{20}{x} \Rightarrow 5 \times x = 7 \times 20 \Rightarrow 5x = 140$

Divide to find x: $x = \frac{140}{5} \Rightarrow x = 28$

bit.ly/37GHQxp

Find more at

Similarity and Ratios

- Two figures are similar if they have the same shape.

- Two or more figures are similar if the corresponding angles are equal, and the corresponding sides are in proportion.

Examples:

Example 1. The following triangles are similar. What is the value of the unknown side?

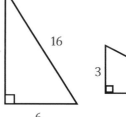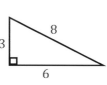

Example 2.

Solution: Find the corresponding sides and write a proportion.

$\frac{8}{16} = \frac{6}{x}$. Now, use the cross product to solve for x:

$\frac{8}{16} = \frac{6}{x} \rightarrow 8 \times x = 16 \times 6 \rightarrow 8x = 96$. Divide both sides by 8. Then: $8x = 96 \rightarrow x = \frac{96}{8} \rightarrow x = 12$

The missing side is 12.

Example 3. Two rectangles are similar. The first is 5 feet wide and 15 feet long. The second is 10 feet wide. What is the length of the second rectangle?

Solution: Let's put x for the length of the second rectangle. Since two rectangles are similar, their corresponding sides are in proportion. Write a proportion and solve for the missing number.

$\frac{5}{10} = \frac{15}{x} \rightarrow 5x = 10 \times 15 \rightarrow 5x = 150 \rightarrow x = \frac{150}{5} = 30$

The length of the second rectangle is 30 feet.

bit.ly/2KKKmcV

Find more at

Chapter 4: Practices

✍ Reduce each ratio.

1) $2:18 = $ ___ : ___

2) $5:35 = $ ___ : ___

3) $8:72 = $ ___ : ___

4) $24:36 = $ ___ : ___

5) $25:40 = $ ___ : ___

6) $40:72 = $ ___ : ___

7) $28:63 = $ ___ : ___

8) $18:81 = $ ___ : ___

9) $13:52 = $ ___ : ___

10) $56:72 = $ ___ : ___

11) $42:63 = $ ___ : ___

12) $32:96 = $ ___ : ___

✍ Solve.

13) Bob has 16 red cards and 20 green cards. What is the ratio of Bob's red cards to his green cards? _____

14) In a party, 34 soft drinks are required for every 20 guests. If there are 260 guests, how many soft drinks are required? _____

15) Sara has 56 blue pens and 28 black pens. What is the ratio of Sara's black pens to her blue pens? _____

16) In Jack's class, 48 of the students are tall and 20 are short. In Michael's class 28 students are tall and 12 students are short. Which class has a higher ratio of tall to short students? _____

17) The price of 6 apples at the Quick Market is $1.52. The price of 5 of the same apples at Walmart is $1.32. Which place is the better buy? _____

18) The bakers at a Bakery can make 180 bagels in 6 hours. How many bagels can they bake in 16 hours? What is that rate per hour? _____

19) You can buy 6 cans of green beans at a supermarket for $3.48. How much does it cost to buy 38 cans of green beans? _____

Effortless Math Education

✍ Solve each proportion.

20) $\dfrac{3}{2} = \dfrac{9}{x} \Rightarrow x =$ _____

21) $\dfrac{7}{2} = \dfrac{x}{4} \Rightarrow x =$ _____

22) $\dfrac{1}{3} = \dfrac{2}{x} \Rightarrow x =$ _____

23) $\dfrac{1}{4} = \dfrac{5}{x} \Rightarrow x =$ _____

24) $\dfrac{9}{6} = \dfrac{x}{2} \Rightarrow x =$ _____

25) $\dfrac{3}{6} = \dfrac{5}{x} \Rightarrow x =$ _____

26) $\dfrac{7}{x} = \dfrac{2}{6} \Rightarrow x =$ _____

27) $\dfrac{2}{x} = \dfrac{4}{10} \Rightarrow x =$ _____

28) $\dfrac{3}{2} = \dfrac{x}{8} \Rightarrow x =$ _____

29) $\dfrac{x}{6} = \dfrac{5}{3} \Rightarrow x =$ _____

30) $\dfrac{3}{9} = \dfrac{5}{x} \Rightarrow x =$ _____

31) $\dfrac{4}{18} = \dfrac{2}{x} \Rightarrow x =$ _____

32) $\dfrac{6}{16} = \dfrac{3}{x} \Rightarrow x =$ _____

33) $\dfrac{2}{5} = \dfrac{x}{20} \Rightarrow x =$ _____

34) $\dfrac{28}{8} = \dfrac{x}{2} \Rightarrow x =$ _____

35) $\dfrac{3}{5} = \dfrac{x}{15} \Rightarrow x =$ _____

36) $\dfrac{2}{7} = \dfrac{x}{14} \Rightarrow x =$ _____

37) $\dfrac{x}{18} = \dfrac{3}{2} \Rightarrow x =$ _____

38) $\dfrac{x}{24} = \dfrac{2}{6} \Rightarrow x =$ _____

39) $\dfrac{5}{x} = \dfrac{4}{20} \Rightarrow x =$ _____

40) $\dfrac{10}{x} = \dfrac{20}{80} \Rightarrow x =$ _____

41) $\dfrac{90}{6} = \dfrac{x}{2} \Rightarrow x =$ _____

✍ Solve each problem.

42) Two rectangles are similar. The first is 8 *feet* wide and 32 *feet* long. The second is 12 *feet* wide. What is the length of the second rectangle?

_____

43) Two rectangles are similar. One is 4.6 *meters* by 7 *meters*. The longer side of the second rectangle is 28 *meters*. What is the other side of the second rectangle? _____

**Effortless
Math
Education**

Chapter 4: Answers

1) $1:9$

2) $1:7$

3) $1:9$

4) $2:3$

5) $5:8$

6) $5:9$

7) $4:9$

8) $2:9$

9) $1:4$

10) $7:9$

11) $2:3$

12) $1:3$

13) $4:5$

14) 442

15) $1:2$

16) Jack's class: $\frac{48}{20} = \frac{12}{5}$ Michael's class: $\frac{28}{12} = \frac{7}{3}$ Jack's class has a higher ratio of tall to short student: $\frac{12}{5} > \frac{7}{3}$

17) Quick market

18) 480, 30 bagels per hour

19) $22.04

20) 6

21) 14

22) 6

23) 20

24) 3

25) 10

26) 21

27) 5

28) 12

29) 10

30) 15

31) 9

32) 8

33) 8

34) 7

35) 9

36) 4

37) 27

38) 8

39) 25

40) 40

41) 30

42) 48 *feet*

43) 18.4 *meters*

Effortless Math Education

CHAPTER

5 Percentage

Math topics that you'll learn in this chapter:

- ☑ Percent Problems
- ☑ Percent of Increase and Decrease
- ☑ Discount, Tax and Tip
- ☑ Simple Interest

Percent Problems

- Percent is a ratio of a number and 100. It always has the same denominator, 100. The percent symbol is "%".

- Percent means "per 100". So, 20% is 20/100.

- In each percent problem, we are looking for the base, or part or the percent.

- Use these equations to find each missing section in a percent problem:

 ❖ Base = Part ÷ Percent

 ❖ Part = Percent × Base

 ❖ Percent = Part ÷ Base

Examples:

Example 1. What is 20% of 40?

Solution: In this problem, we have percent (20%) and base (40) and we are looking for the "part". Use this formula: *part = percent × base*.

Then: $part = 20\% \times 40 = \frac{20}{100} \times 40 = 0.20 \times 40 = 8$. The answer: 20% of 40 is 8.

Example 2. 25 is what percent of 500?

Solution: In this problem, we are looking for the percent. Use this equation: *Percent = Part ÷ Base → Percent = 25 ÷ 500 = 0.05 = 5%*.
Then: 25 is 5 percent of 500.

Percent of Increase and Decrease

- Percent of change (increase or decrease) is a mathematical concept that represents the degree of change over time.

- To find the percentage of increase or decrease:

  1. New Number – Original Number
  2. The result ÷ Original Number × 100

- Or use this formula: Percent of change $= \frac{new\ number - original\ number}{original\ number} \times 100$

- Note: If your answer is a negative number, then this is a percentage decrease. If it is positive, then this is a percentage increase.

Examples:

Example 1. The price of a shirt increases from \$30 to \$40. What is the percentage increase?

Solution: First, find the difference: $40 - 30 = 10$

Then: $10 \div 30 \times 100 = \frac{10}{30} \times 100 = 33.33$. The percentage increase is 33.33. It means that the price of the shirt increased by 33.33%.

Example 2. The price of a table increased from \$20 to \$50. What is the percent of increase?

Solution: Use percentage formula:

$Percent\ of\ change = \frac{new\ number - original\ number}{original\ number} \times 100 =$

$\frac{50-20}{20} \times 100 = \frac{30}{20} \times 100 = 1.5 \times 100 = 150$. The percentage increase is 150. It means that the price of the table increased by 150%.

bit.ly/3pgPQes

Discount, Tax and Tip

- To find the discount: Multiply the regular price by the rate of discount

- To find the selling price: Original price – discount

- To find tax: Multiply the tax rate to the taxable amount (income, property value, etc.)

- To find the tip, multiply the rate to the selling price.

Examples:

Example 1. With an 20% discount, Ella saved $50 on a dress. What was the original price of the dress?

Solution: let x be the original price of the dress. Then: 20 % *of* $x = 50$. Write an equation and solve for x: $0.20 \times x = 50 \rightarrow x = \frac{50}{0.20} = 250$. The original price of the dress was $250.

Example 2. Sophia purchased a new computer for a price of $820 at the Apple Store. What is the total amount her credit card is charged if the sales tax is 5%?

Solution: The taxable amount is $820, and the tax rate is 5%. Then: $Tax = 0.05 \times 820 = 41$
Final price = *Selling price* + *Tax* → *final price* = $820 + $41 = $861

Example 3. Nicole and her friends went out to eat at a restaurant. If their bill was $60.00 and they gave their server a 15% tip, how much did they pay altogether?

Solution: First, find the tip. To find the tip, multiply the rate to the bill amount. $Tip = 60 \times 0.15 = 9$. The final price is: $60 + $9 = $69

Simple Interest

- Simple Interest: The charge for borrowing money or the return for lending it.

- Simple interest is calculated on the initial amount (principal).

- To solve a simple interest problem, use this formula:

Interest = principal × rate × time $(I = p \times r \times t = prt)$

Examples:

Example 1. Find simple interest for $200 investment at 5% for 3 years.

Solution: Use Interest formula:
$I = prt$ ($P = \$200$, r = 5% = $\frac{5}{100}$ = 0.05 and $t = 3$)
Then: $I = 200 \times 0.05 \times 3 = \$30$

Example 2. Find simple interest for $1,200 at 8% for 6 years.

Solution: Use Interest formula:
$I = prt$ ($P = \$1,200$, r = 8% = $\frac{8}{100}$ = 0.08 and $t = 6$)
Then: $I = 1,200 \times 0.08 \times 6 = \$576$

Example 3. Andy received a student loan to pay for his educational expenses this year. What is the interest on the loan if he borrowed $4,500 at 6% for 5 years?

Solution: Use Interest formula: $I = prt$. $P = \$4,500$, r = 6% = 0.06 and $t = 5$
Then: $I = 4,500 \times 0.06 \times 5 = \$1,350$

Example 4. Bob is starting his own small business. He borrowed $20,000 from the bank at a 8% rate for 6 months. Find the interest Bob will pay on this loan.

Solution: Use Interest formula:
$I = prt$. $P = \$20,000$, r = 8% = 0.08 and $t = 0.5$ (6 months is half year). Then: $I = 20,000 \times 0.08 \times 0.5 = \$800$

bit.ly/3nJli3D

Find more at

Chapter 5: Practices

✍ Solve each problem.

1) What is 15% of 60? ____

2) What is 55% of 800? ____

3) What is 22% of 120? ____

4) What is 18% of 40? ____

5) 90 is what percent of 200? ____%

6) 30 is what percent of 150? ____%

7) 14 is what percent of 250? ____%

8) 60 is what percent of 300? ____%

9) 30 is 120 percent of what number? ____

10) 120 is 20 percent of what number? ____

11) 15 is 5 percent of what number? ____

12) 22 is 20% of what number? ____

✍ Solve each problem.

13) Bob got a raise, and his hourly wage increased from $15 to $21. What is the percent increase? _____ %

14) The price of a pair of shoes increases from $32 to $36. What is the percent increase? ___ %

15) At a Coffee Shop, the price of a cup of coffee increased from $1.35 to $1.62. What is the percent increase in the cost of the coffee? _____ %

16) A $45 shirt now selling for $36 is discounted by what percent? _____ %

17) Joe scored 30 out of 35 marks in Algebra, 20 out of 30 marks in science and 58 out of 70 marks in mathematics. In which subject his percentage of marks is best? _____

18) Emma purchased a computer for $420. The computer is regularly priced at $480. What was the percent discount Emma received on the computer? _____

19) A chemical solution contains 15% alcohol. If there is 54 ml of alcohol, what is the volume of the solution? _____

✍ Find the selling price of each item.

20) Original price of a computer: $600

   Tax: 8%, Selling price: $_____

21) Original price of a laptop: $450

   Tax: 10%, Selling price: $_____

22) Nicolas hired a moving company. The company charged $500 for its services, and Nicolas gives the movers a 14% tip. How much does Nicolas tip the movers? $_____

23) Mason has lunch at a restaurant and the cost of his meal is $40. Mason wants to leave a 20% tip. What is Mason's total bill, including tip? $_____

✍ Determine the simple interest for the following loans.

24) $1,000 *at* 5% *for* 4 *years.* $___

25) $400 *at* 3% *for* 5 *years.* $___

26) $240 *at* 4% *for* 3 *years.* $___

27) $500 at 4.5% for 6 years. $___

✍ Solve.

28) A new car, valued at $20,000, depreciates at 8% per year. What is the value of the car one year after purchase? $_____

29) Sara puts $7,000 into an investment yielding 3% annual simple interest; she left the money in for five years. How much interest does Sara get at the end of those five years? $_____

Effortless Math Education

Chapter 5: Answers

1) 9

2) 440

3) 26.4

4) 7.2

5) 45%

6) 20%

7) 5.6%

8) 20%

9) 25

10) 600

11) 300

12) 110

13) 40%

14) 12.5%

15) 20%

16) 20%

17) Algebra

18) 12.5%

19) 360 ml

20) $648.00

21) $495.00

22) $70.00

23) $48.00

24) $200.00

25) $60.00

26) $28.80

27) $135.00

28) $18.400

29) $1,050

CHAPTER

6 Exponents and Variables

Math topics that you'll learn in this chapter:

- ☑ Multiplication Property of Exponents
- ☑ Division Property of Exponents
- ☑ Powers of Products and Quotients
- ☑ Zero and Negative Exponents
- ☑ Negative Exponents and Negative Bases
- ☑ Scientific Notation
- ☑ Radicals

Multiplication Property of Exponents

- Exponents are shorthand for repeated multiplication of the same number by itself. For example, instead of 2×2, we can write 2^2. For $3 \times 3 \times 3 \times 3$, we can write 3^4

- In algebra, a variable is a letter used to stand for a number. The most common letters are: x, y, z, a, b, c, m, and n.

- Exponent's rules: $x^a \times x^b = x^{a+b}$, $\dfrac{x^a}{x^b} = x^{a-b}$

$$(x^a)^b = x^{a \times b} \qquad\qquad (xy)^a = x^a \times y^a \qquad\qquad \left(\dfrac{a}{b}\right)^c = \dfrac{a^c}{b^c}$$

Examples:

Example 1. Multiply. $2x^2 \times 3x^4$

Solution: Use Exponent's rules: $x^a \times x^b = x^{a+b} \rightarrow x^2 \times x^4 = x^{2+4} = x^6$
Then: $2x^2 \times 3x^4 = 6x^6$

Example 2. Simplify. $(x^4 y^2)^2$

Solution: Use Exponent's rules: $(x^a)^b = x^{a \times b}$.
Then: $(x^4 y^2)^2 = x^{4 \times 2} y^{2 \times 2} = x^8 y^4$

Example 3. Multiply. $5x^8 \times 6x^5$

Solution: Use Exponent's rules: $x^a \times x^b = x^{a+b} \rightarrow x^8 \times x^5 = x^{8+5} = x^{13}$
Then: $5x^8 \times 6x^5 = 30x^{13}$

Example 4. Simplify. $(x^4 y^7)^3$

Solution: Use Exponent's rules: $(x^a)^b = x^{a \times b}$.
Then: $(x^4 y^7)^3 = x^{4 \times 3} y^{7 \times 3} = x^{12} y^{21}$

Division Property of Exponents

- Exponents are shorthand for repeated multiplication of the same number by itself. For example, instead of 3×3, we can write 3^2. For $2 \times 2 \times 2$, we can write 2^3

- For division of exponents use following formulas:

$$\frac{x^a}{x^b} = x^{a-b} \, , x \neq 0, \frac{x^a}{x^b} = \frac{1}{x^{b-a}} \, , x \neq 0, \qquad \frac{1}{x^b} = x^{-b}$$

Examples:

Example 1. Simplify. $\frac{16x^3y}{2xy^2} =$

Solution: First, cancel the common factor: $2 \rightarrow \frac{16x^3y}{2xy^2} = \frac{8x^3y}{xy^2}$

Use Exponent's rules: $\frac{x^a}{x^b} = x^{a-b} \rightarrow \frac{x^3}{x} = x^{3-1} = x^2$ and $\frac{y}{y^2} = \frac{1}{y^{2-1}} = \frac{1}{y}$

Then: $\frac{16x^3y}{2xy^2} = \frac{8x^2}{y}$

Example 2. Simplify. $\frac{24x^8}{3x^6} =$

Solution: Use Exponent's rules: $\frac{x^a}{x^b} = x^{b-a} \rightarrow \frac{x^8}{x^6} = x^{8-6} = x^2$

Then: $\frac{24x^8}{3x^6} = 8x^2$

Example 3. Simplify. $\frac{7x^4y^2}{28x^3y} =$

Solution: First, cancel the common factor: $7 \rightarrow \frac{x^4y^2}{4x^3y}$

Use Exponent's rules: $\frac{x^a}{x^b} = x^{a-b} \rightarrow \frac{x^4}{x^3} = x^{4-3} = x$ and $\frac{y^2}{y} = y$

Then: $\frac{7x^4y^2}{28x^3y} = \frac{xy}{4}$

bit.ly/37JAclZ

Find more at

Powers of Products and Quotients

- Exponents are shorthand for repeated multiplication of the same number by itself. For example, instead of $2 \times 2 \times 2$, we can write 2^3. For $3 \times 3 \times 3 \times 3$, we can write 3^4

- For any nonzero numbers a and b and any integer x, $(ab)^x = a^x \times b^x$ and $\left(\frac{a}{b}\right)^c = \frac{a^c}{b^c}$

Examples:

Example 1. Simplify. $(3x^3y^2)^2$

Solution: Use Exponent's rules: $(x^a)^b = x^{a \times b}$
$(3x^3y^2)^2 = (3)^2(x^3)^2(y^2)^2 = 9x^{3 \times 2}y^{2 \times 2} = 9x^6y^4$

Example 2. Simplify. $\left(\frac{2x^3}{3x^2}\right)^2$

Solution: First, cancel the common factor: $x \rightarrow \left(\frac{2x^3}{3x^2}\right) = \left(\frac{2x}{3}\right)^2$
Use Exponent's rules: $\left(\frac{a}{b}\right)^c = \frac{a^c}{b^c}$, Then: $\left(\frac{2x}{3}\right)^2 = \frac{(2x)^2}{(3)^2} = \frac{4x^2}{9}$

Example 3. Simplify. $\left(-4x^3y^5\right)^2$

Solution: Use Exponent's rules: $(x^a)^b = x^{a \times b}$
$$\left(-4x^3y^5\right)^2 = (-4)^2(x^3)^2\left(y^5\right)^2 = 16x^{3 \times 2}y^{5 \times 2} = 16x^6y^{10}$$

Example 4. Simplify. $\left(\frac{5x}{4x^2}\right)^2$

Solution: First, cancel the common factor: $x \rightarrow \left(\frac{5x}{4x^2}\right)^2 = \left(\frac{5}{4x}\right)^2$
Use Exponent's rules: $\left(\frac{a}{b}\right)^c = \frac{a^c}{b^c}$, Then: $\left(\frac{5}{4x}\right)^2 = \frac{5^2}{(4x)^2} = \frac{25}{16x^2}$

Zero and Negative Exponents

- Zero-Exponent Rule: $a^0 = 1$, this means that anything raised to the zero power is 1. For example: $(5xy)^0 = 1$

- A negative exponent simply means that the base is on the wrong side of the fraction line, so you need to flip the base to the other side. For instance, "x^{-2}" (pronounced as "ecks to the minus two") just means "x^2" but underneath, as in $\frac{1}{x^2}$.

Examples:

Example 1. Evaluate. $\left(\frac{4}{5}\right)^{-2} =$

Solution: Use negative exponent's rule: $\left(\frac{x^a}{x^b}\right)^{-2} = \left(\frac{x^b}{x^a}\right)^2 \rightarrow \left(\frac{4}{5}\right)^{-2} = \left(\frac{5}{4}\right)^2 =$
Then: $\left(\frac{5}{4}\right)^2 = \frac{5^2}{4^2} = \frac{25}{16}$

Example 2. Evaluate. $\left(\frac{3}{2}\right)^{-3} =$

Solution: Use negative exponent's rule: $\left(\frac{x^a}{x^b}\right)^{-3} = \left(\frac{x^b}{x^a}\right)^3 \rightarrow \left(\frac{3}{2}\right)^{-3} = \left(\frac{2}{3}\right)^3 =$
Then: $\left(\frac{2}{3}\right)^3 = \frac{2^3}{3^3} = \frac{8}{27}$

Example 3. Evaluate. $\left(\frac{a}{b}\right)^0 =$

Solution: Use zero-exponent Rule: $a^0 = 1$
Then: $\left(\frac{a}{b}\right)^0 = 1$

Example 4. Evaluate. $\left(\frac{4}{7}\right)^{-1} =$

Solution: Use negative exponent's rule: $\left(\frac{x^a}{x^b}\right)^{-1} = \left(\frac{x^b}{x^a}\right)^1 \rightarrow \left(\frac{4}{7}\right)^{-1} = \left(\frac{7}{4}\right)^1 = \frac{7}{4}$

bit.ly/3rnkh4v

Find more at

Negative Exponents and Negative Bases

- A negative exponent is the reciprocal of that number with a positive exponent. $(3)^{-2} = \frac{1}{3^2}$

- To simplify a negative exponent, make the power positive!

- The parenthesis is important! -5^{-2} is not the same as $(-5)^{-2}$

$$-5^{-2} = -\frac{1}{5^2} \quad \text{and} \quad (-5)^{-2} = +\frac{1}{5^2}$$

Examples:

Example 1. Simplify. $\left(\frac{2a}{3c}\right)^{-2} =$

Solution: Use negative exponent's rule: $\left(\frac{x^a}{x^b}\right)^{-2} = \left(\frac{x^b}{x^a}\right)^{2} \rightarrow \left(\frac{2a}{3c}\right)^{-2} = \left(\frac{3c}{2a}\right)^{2}$

Now use exponent's rule: $\left(\frac{a}{b}\right)^c = \frac{a^c}{b^c} \rightarrow = \left(\frac{3c}{2a}\right)^{2} = \frac{3^2c^2}{2^2a^2}$

Then: $\frac{3^2c^2}{2^2a^2} = \frac{9c^2}{4a^2}$

Example 2. Simplify. $\left(\frac{x}{4y}\right)^{-3} =$

Solution: Use negative exponent's rule: $\left(\frac{x^a}{x^b}\right)^{-3} = \left(\frac{x^b}{x^a}\right)^{3} \rightarrow \left(\frac{x}{4y}\right)^{-3} = \left(\frac{4y}{x}\right)^{3}$

Now use exponent's rule: $\left(\frac{a}{b}\right)^c = \frac{a^c}{b^c} \rightarrow \left(\frac{4y}{x}\right)^{3} = \frac{4^3y^3}{x^3} = \frac{64y^3}{x^3}$

Example 3. Simplify. $\left(\frac{5a}{2c}\right)^{-2} =$

Solution: Use negative exponent's rule: $\left(\frac{x^a}{x^b}\right)^{-2} = \left(\frac{x^b}{x^a}\right)^{2} \rightarrow \left(\frac{5a}{2c}\right)^{-2} = \left(\frac{2c}{5a}\right)^{2}$

Now use exponent's rule: $\left(\frac{a}{b}\right)^c = \frac{a^c}{b^c} \rightarrow = \left(\frac{2c}{5a}\right)^{2} = \frac{2^2c^2}{5^2a^2}$

Then: $\frac{2^2c^2}{5^2a^2} = \frac{4c^2}{25a^2}$

Scientific Notation

- Scientific notation is used to write very big or very small numbers in decimal form.

- In scientific notation, all numbers are written in the form of: $m \times 10^n$, where m is greater than 1 and less than 10.

- To convert a number from scientific notation to standard form, move the decimal point to the left (if the exponent of ten is a negative number), or to the right (if the exponent is positive).

Examples:

Example 1. Write 0.00024 in scientific notation.

Solution: First, move the decimal point to the right so you have a number between 1 and 10. That number is 2.4. Now, determine how many places the decimal moved in step 1 by the power of 10. We moved the decimal point 4 digits to the right. Then: $10^{-4} \rightarrow$ When the decimal moved to the right, the exponent is negative. Then: $0.00024 = 2.4 \times 10^{-4}$

Example 2. Write 3.8×10^{-5} in standard notation.

Solution: $10^{-5} \rightarrow$ When the decimal moved to the right, the exponent is negative. Then: $3.8 \times 10^{-5} = 0.000038$

Example 3. Write 0.00031 in scientific notation.

Solution: First, move the decimal point to the right so you have a number between 1 and 10. Then: $m = 3.1$, Now, determine how many places the decimal moved in step 1 by the power of 10.
$10^{-4} \rightarrow$ Then: $0.00031 = 3.1 \times 10^{-4}$

Example 4. Write 6.2×10^5 in standard notation.

Solution: $10^5 \rightarrow$ The exponent is positive 5. Then, move the decimal point to the right five digits. (remember 6.2 = 6.20000),
Then: $6.2 \times 10^5 = 620000$

Radicals

- If n is a positive integer and x is a real number, then: $\sqrt[n]{x} = x^{\frac{1}{n}}$,

$$\sqrt[n]{xy} = x^{\frac{1}{n}} \times y^{\frac{1}{n}}, \ \sqrt[n]{\frac{x}{y}} = \frac{x^{\frac{1}{n}}}{y^{\frac{1}{n}}}, \text{ and } \sqrt[n]{x} \times \sqrt[n]{y} = \sqrt[n]{xy}$$

- A square root of x is a number r whose square is: $r^2 = x$ (r is a square root of x)

- To add and subtract radicals, we need to have the same values under the radical. For example: $\sqrt{3} + \sqrt{3} = 2\sqrt{3}$, $3\sqrt{5} - \sqrt{5} = 2\sqrt{5}$

Examples:

Example 1. Find the square root of $\sqrt{121}$.

Solution: First, factor the number: $121 = 11^2$, Then: $\sqrt{121} = \sqrt{11^2}$,
Now use radical rule: $\sqrt[n]{a^n} = a$. Then: $\sqrt{121} = \sqrt{11^2} = 11$

Example 2. Evaluate. $\sqrt{4} \times \sqrt{16} =$

Solution: Find the values of $\sqrt{4}$ and $\sqrt{16}$. Then: $\sqrt{4} \times \sqrt{16} = 2 \times 4 = 8$

Example 3. Solve. $5\sqrt{2} + 9\sqrt{2}$.

Solution: Since we have the same values under the radical, we can add these two radicals: $5\sqrt{2} + 9\sqrt{2} = 14\sqrt{2}$

Example 4. Evaluate. $\sqrt{2} \times \sqrt{50} =$

Solution: Use this radical rule: $\sqrt[n]{x} \times \sqrt[n]{y} = \sqrt[n]{xy} \rightarrow \sqrt{2} \times \sqrt{50} = \sqrt{100}$
The square root of 100 is 10. Then: $\sqrt{2} \times \sqrt{50} = \sqrt{100} = 10$

Chapter 6: Practices

✎ Find the products.

1) $x^2 \times 4xy^2 =$

2) $3x^2y \times 5x^3y^2 =$

3) $6x^4y^2 \times x^2y^3 =$

4) $7xy^3 \times 2x^2y =$

5) $-5x^5y^5 \times x^3y^2 =$

6) $-8x^3y^2 \times 3x^3y^2 =$

7) $-6x^2y^6 \times 5x^4y^2 =$

8) $-3x^3y^3 \times 2x^3y^2 =$

9) $-6x^5y^3 \times 4x^4y^3 =$

10) $-2x^4y^3 \times 5x^6y^2 =$

11) $-7y^6 \times 3x^6y^3 =$

12) $-9x^4 \times 2x^4y^2 =$

✎ Simplify.

13) $\dfrac{5^3 \times 5^4}{5^9 \times 5} =$

14) $\dfrac{3^3 \times 3^2}{7^2 \times 7} =$

15) $\dfrac{15x^5}{5x^3} =$

16) $\dfrac{16x^3}{4x^5} =$

17) $\dfrac{72y^2}{8x^3y^6} =$

18) $\dfrac{10x^3y^4}{50x^2y^3} =$

19) $\dfrac{13y^2}{52x^4y^4} =$

20) $\dfrac{50xy^3}{200x^3y^4} =$

21) $\dfrac{48x^2}{56x^2y^2} =$

22) $\dfrac{81y^6x}{54x^4y^3} =$

✎ Solve.

23) $(x^3y^3)^2 =$

24) $(3x^3y^4)^3 =$

25) $(4x \times 6xy^3)^2 =$

26) $(5x \times 2y^3)^3 =$

27) $\left(\dfrac{9x}{x^3}\right)^2 =$

28) $(\dfrac{3y}{18y^2})^2 =$

29) $\left(\dfrac{3x^2y^3}{24x^4y^2}\right)^3 =$

30) $\left(\dfrac{26x^5y^3}{52x^3y^5}\right)^2 =$

31) $\left(\dfrac{18x^7y^4}{72x^5y^2}\right)^2 =$

32) $\left(\dfrac{12x^6y^4}{48x^5y^3}\right)^2 =$

Effortless
Math
Education

✎ **Evaluate each expression. (Zero and Negative Exponents)**

33) $\left(\frac{1}{4}\right)^{-2} =$

34) $\left(\frac{1}{3}\right)^{-2} =$

35) $\left(\frac{1}{7}\right)^{-3} =$

36) $\left(\frac{2}{5}\right)^{-3} =$

37) $\left(\frac{2}{3}\right)^{-3} =$

38) $\left(\frac{3}{5}\right)^{-4} =$

✎ **Write each expression with positive exponents.**

39) $x^{-7} =$

40) $3y^{-5} =$

41) $15y^{-3} =$

42) $-20x^{-4} =$

43) $12a^{-3}b^5 =$

44) $25a^3b^{-4}c^{-3} =$

45) $-4x^5y^{-3}z^{-6} =$

46) $\frac{18y}{x^3y^{-2}} =$

47) $\frac{20a^{-2}b}{-12c^{-4}}$

✎ **Write each number in scientific notation.**

48) $0.00412 =$

49) $0.000053 =$

50) $66,000 =$

51) $72,000,000 =$

✎ **Evaluate.**

52) $\sqrt{8} \times \sqrt{8} =$ ....

53) $\sqrt{36} - \sqrt{9} =$ ....

54) $\sqrt{81} + \sqrt{16} =$ ....

55) $\sqrt{4} \times \sqrt{25} =$ ....

56) $\sqrt{2} \times \sqrt{32} =$ ....

57) $4\sqrt{3} + 5\sqrt{3} =$ ....

Effortless
Math
Education

Effortless

Math

Education

Chapter 6: Answers

1) $4x^3y^2$

2) $15x^5y^3$

3) $6x^6y^5$

4) $14x^3y^4$

5) $-5x^8y^7$

6) $-24x^6y^4$

7) $-30x^6y^8$

8) $-6x^6y^5$

9) $-24x^9y^6$

10) $-10x^{10}y^5$

11) $-21x^6y^9$

12) $-18x^8y^2$

13) $\frac{1}{125}$

14) $\frac{243}{343}$

15) $3x^2$

16) $\frac{4}{x^2}$

17) $\frac{9}{x^3y^4}$

18) $\frac{xy}{5}$

19) $\frac{1}{4x^4y^2}$

20) $\frac{1}{4x^2y}$

21) $\frac{6}{7y^2}$

22) $\frac{3y^3}{2x^3}$

23) x^6y^6

24) $27x^9y^{12}$

25) $576x^4y^6$

26) $1,000x^3y^9$

27) $\frac{81}{x^4}$

28) $\frac{1}{36y^2}$

29) $\frac{y^3}{512x^6}$

30) $\frac{x^4}{4y^4}$

31) $\frac{x^4y^4}{16}$

32) $\frac{x^2y^2}{16}$

33) 16

34) 9

35) 343

36) $\frac{125}{8}$

37) $\frac{27}{8}$

38) $\frac{625}{81}$

39) $\frac{1}{x^7}$

40) $\frac{3}{y^5}$

41) $\frac{15}{y^3}$

42) $-\frac{20}{x^4}$

43) $\frac{12b^5}{a^3}$

44) $\frac{25a^3}{b^4c^3}$

45) $-\frac{4x^5}{y^3z^6}$

46) $\frac{18y^3}{x^3}$

47) $-\frac{5bc^4}{3a^2}$

48) 4.12×10^{-3}

49) 5.3×10^{-5}

50) 6.6×10^4

51) 7.2×10^7

52) 8

53) 3

54) 13

55) 10

56) 8

57) $9\sqrt{3}$

7 Expressions and Variables

Math topics that you'll learn in this chapter:

- ☑ Simplifying Variable Expressions
- ☑ Simplifying Polynomial Expressions
- ☑ The Distributive Property
- ☑ Evaluating One Variable
- ☑ Evaluating Two Variables

Simplifying Variable Expressions

- In algebra, a variable is a letter used to stand for a number. The most common letters are $x, y, z, a, b, c, m,$ and n.

- An algebraic expression is an expression that contains integers, variables, and math operations such as addition, subtraction, multiplication, division, etc.

- In an expression, we can combine "like" terms. (values with same variable and same power)

Examples:

Example 1. Simplify. $(4x + 2x + 4) =$

Solution: In this expression, there are three terms: $4x, 2x,$ and 4. Two terms are "like terms": $4x$ and $2x$. Combine like terms. $4x + 2x = 6x$. Then: $(4x + 2x + 4) = 6x + 4$ (*remember you cannot combine variables and numbers.*)

Example 2. Simplify. $-2x^2 - 5x + 4x^2 - 9 =$

Solution: Combine "like" terms: $-2x^2 + 4x^2 = 2x^2$.
Then: $-2x^2 - 5x + 4x^2 - 9 = 2x^2 - 5x - 9$.

Example 3. Simplify. $(-8 + 6x^2 + 3x^2 + 9x) =$

Solution: Combine like terms. Then:
$(-8 + 6x^2 + 3x^2 + 9x) = 9x^2 + 9x - 8$

Example 4. Simplify. $-10x + 6x^2 - 3x + 9x^2 =$

Solution: Combine "like" terms: $-10x - 3x = -13x$, and $6x^2 + 9x^2 = 15x^2$
Then: $-10x + 6x^2 - 3x + 9x^2 = -13x + 15x^2$. Write in standard form (biggest powers first): $-13x + 15x^2 = 15x^2 - 13x$

Simplifying Polynomial Expressions

- In mathematics, a polynomial is an expression consisting of variables and coefficients that involves only the operations of addition, subtraction, multiplication, and non–negative integer exponents of variables. $P(x) = a_n x^n + a_{n-1} x^{n-1} + \dots + a_2 x^2 + a_1 x + a_0$

- Polynomials must always be simplified as much as possible. It means you must add together any like terms. (values with same variable and same power)

Examples:

Example 1. Simplify this Polynomial Expressions. $3x^2 - 6x^3 - 2x^3 + 4x^4$

Solution: Combine "like" terms: $-6x^3 - 2x^3 = -8x^3$
Then: $3x^2 - 6x^3 - 2x^3 + 4x^4 = 3x^2 - 8x^3 + 4x^4$
Now, write the expression in standard form: $4x^4 - 8x^3 + 3x^2$

Example 2. Simplify this expression. $(-5x^2 + 2x^3) - (3x^3 - 6x^2) =$

Solution: First, use distributive property: → multiply $(-)$ into $(3x^3 - 6x^2)$
$(-5x^2 + 2x^3) - (3x^3 - 6x^2) = -5x^2 + 2x^3 - 3x^3 + 6x^2$
Then combine "like" terms: $-5x^2 + 2x^3 - 3x^3 + 6x^2 = x^2 - x^3$
And write in standard form: $x^2 - x^3 = -x^3 + x^2$

Example 3. Simplify. $3x^3 - 9x^4 - 8x^2 + 12x^4 =$

Solution: Combine "like" terms:
$-9x^4 + 12x^4 = 3x^4$
Then: $3x^3 - 9x^4 - 8x^2 + 12x^4 = 3x^3 + 3x^4 - 8x^2$
And write in standard form: $3x^3 + 3x^4 - 8x^2 = 3x^4 + 3x^3 - 8x^2$

The Distributive Property

- The distributive property (or the distributive property of multiplication over addition and subtraction) simplifies and solves expressions in the form of: $a(b + c)$ or $a(b - c)$

- The distributive property is multiplying a term outside the parentheses by the terms inside.

- Distributive Property rule: $a(b + c) = ab + ac$

Examples:

Example 1. Simply using the distributive property. $(-2)(x + 3)$

Solution: Use Distributive Property rule: $a(b + c) = ab + ac$
$(-2)(x + 3) = (-2 \times x) + (-2) \times (3) = -2x - 6$

Example 2. Simply. $(-5)(-2x - 6)$

Solution: Use Distributive Property rule: $a(b + c) = ab + ac$
$(-5)(-2x - 6) = (-5 \times -2x) + (-5) \times (-6) = 10x + 30$

Example 3. Simply. $(7)(2x - 8) - 12x$

Solution: First, simplify $(7)(2x - 8)$ using the distributive property.
Then: $(7)(2x - 8) = 14x - 56$
Now combine like terms: $(7)(2x - 8) - 12x = 14x - 56 - 12x$
In this expression, $14x$ and $-12x$ are "like terms" and we can combine them.
$14x - 12x = 2x$. Then: $14x - 56 - 12x = 2x - 56$

bit.ly/38qCaXs

Find more at

Evaluating One Variable

- To evaluate one variable expression, find the variable and substitute a number for that variable.

- Perform the arithmetic operations.

Examples:

Example 1. Calculate this expression for $x = 2$. $8 + 2x$

Solution: First, substitute 2 for x

Then: $8 + 2x = 8 + 2(2)$

Now, use order of operation to find the answer: $8 + 2(2) = 8 + 4 = 12$

Example 2. Evaluate this expression for $x = -1$. $4x - 8$

Solution: First, substitute -1 for x,

Then: $4x - 8 = 4(-1) - 8$

Now, use order of operation to find the answer: $4(-1) - 8 = -4 - 8 = -12$

Example 3. Find the value of this expression when $x = 4$. $16 - 5x$

Solution: First, substitute 4 for x,

Then: $16 - 5x = 16 - 5(4) = 16 - 20 = -4$

Example 4. Solve this expression for $x = -3$. $15 + 7x$

Solution: Substitute -3 for x,

Then: $15 + 7x = 15 + 7(-3) = 15 - 21 = -6$

bit.ly/3ppujQZ

Find more at

Evaluating Two Variables

- To evaluate an algebraic expression, substitute a number for each variable.

- Perform the arithmetic operations to find the value of the expression.

Examples:

Example 1. Calculate this expression for a $= 2$ and $b = -1$. $4a - 3b$

Solution: First, substitute 2 for a, and -1 for b ,

*T*hen: $4a - 3b = 4(2) - 3(-1)$

Now, use order of operation to find the answer: $4(2) - 3(-1) = 8 + 3 = 11$

Example 2. Evaluate this expression for $x = -2$ and $y = 2$. $3x + 6y$

Solution: Substitute -2 for x, and 2 for y ,

Then: $3x + 6y = 3(-2) + 6(2) = -6 + 12 = 6$

Example 3. Find the value of this expression $2(6a - 5b)$ when $a = -1$ and $b = 4$.

Solution: Substitute -1 for a, and 4 for b ,

Then: $2(6a - 5b) = 12a - 10b = 12(-1) - 10(4) = -12 - 40 = -52$

Example 4. Solve this expression. $-7x - 2y$, $x = 4$, $y = -3$

Solution: Substitute 4 for x, and -3 for y and simplify.

Then: $-7x - 2y = -7(4) - 2(-3) = -28 + 6 = -22$

Chapter 7: Practices

✎ Simplify each expression.

1) $(3 + 4x - 1) =$

2) $(-5 - 2x + 7) =$

3) $(12x - 5x - 4) =$

4) $(-16x + 24x - 9) =$

5) $(6x + 5 - 15x) =$

6) $2 + 5x - 8x - 6 =$

7) $5x + 10 - 3x - 22 =$

8) $-5 - 3x^2 - 6 + 4x =$

9) $-6 + 9x^2 - 3 + x =$

10) $5x^2 + 3x - 10x - 3 =$

11) $4x^2 - 2x - 6x + 5 - 8 =$

12) $3x^2 - 5x - 7x + 2 - 4 =$

13) $9x^2 - x - 5x + 3 - 9 =$

14) $2x^2 - 7x - 3x^2 + 4x + 6 =$

✎ Simplify each polynomial.

15) $5x^2 + 3x^3 - 9x^2 + 2x =$

16) $8x^4 + 2x^5 - 7x^4 + 3x^2 =$

17) $15x^3 + 11x - 5x^2 - 9x^3 =$

18) $(7x^3 - 3x^2) + (5x^2 - 13x) =$

19) $(12x^4 + 6x^3) + (x^3 - 5x^4) =$

20) $(15x^5 - 8x^3) - (4x^3 + x^2) =$

21) $(14x^4 + 7x^3) - (x^3 - 24) =$

22) $(20x^4 + 6x^3) - (-x^3 - 2x^4) =$

23) $(x^2 + 9x^3) + (-22x^2 + 6x^3) =$

24) $(4x^4 - 2x^3) + (-5x^3 - 8x^4) =$

Effortless
Math
Education

✍ Use the distributive property to simply each expression.

25) $2(6 + x) =$ _____

26) $5(3 - 2x) =$ _____

27) $7(1 - 5x) =$ _____

28) $(3 - 4x)7 =$ _____

29) $6(2 - 3x) =$ _____

30) $(-1)(-9 + x) =$ _____

31) $(-6)(3x - 2) =$ _____

32) $(-x + 12)(-4) =$ _____

33) $(-2)(1 - 6x) =$ _____

34) $(-5x - 3)(-8) =$ _____

✍ Evaluate each expression using the value given.

35) $x = 4 \rightarrow 10 - x =$ ____

36) $x = 6 \rightarrow x + 8 =$ ____

37) $x = 3 \rightarrow 2x - 6 =$ ____

38) $x = 2 \rightarrow 10 - 4x =$ ____

39) $x = 7 \rightarrow 8x - 3 =$ ____

40) $x = 9 \rightarrow 20 - 2x =$ ____

41) $x = 5 \rightarrow 10x - 30 =$ ___

42) $x = -6 \rightarrow 5 - x =$ ____

43) $x = -3 \rightarrow 22 - 3x =$ ____

44) $x = -7 \rightarrow 10 - 9x =$ ____

45) $x = -10 \rightarrow 40 - 3x =$ ____

46) $x = -2 \rightarrow 20x - 5 =$ ____

47) $x = -5 \rightarrow -10x - 8 =$ ___

48) $x = -4 \rightarrow -1 - 4x =$ ___

✍ Evaluate each expression using the values given.

49) $x = 2, y = 1 \rightarrow 2x + 7y =$ _____

50) $a = 3, b = 5 \rightarrow 3a - 5b =$ _____

51) $x = 6, y = 2 \rightarrow 3x - 2y + 8 =$ _____

52) $a = -2, b = 3 \rightarrow -5a + 2b + 6 =$ _____

53) $x = -4, y = -3 \rightarrow -4x + 10 - 8y =$ _____

Effortless Math Education

Effortless
Math
Education

Chapter 7: Answers

1) $4x + 2$

2) $-2x + 2$

3) $7x - 4$

4) $8x - 9$

5) $-9x + 5$

6) $-3x - 4$

7) $2x - 12$

8) $-3x^2 + 4x - 11$

9) $9x^2 + x - 9$

10) $5x^2 - 7x - 3$

11) $4x^2 - 8x - 3$

12) $3x^2 - 12x - 2$

13) $9x^2 - 6x - 6$

14) $-x^2 - 3x + 6$

15) $3x^3 - 4x^2 + 2x$

16) $2x^5 + x^4 + 3x^2$

17) $6x^3 - 5x^2 + 11x$

18) $7x^3 + 2x^2 - 13x$

19) $7x^4 + 7x^3$

20) $15x^5 - 12x^3 - x^2$

21) $14x^4 + 6x^3 + 24$

22) $22x^4 + 7x^3$

23) $15x^3 - 21x^2$

24) $-4x^4 - 7x^3$

25) $2x + 12$

26) $-10x + 15$

27) $-35x + 7$

28) $-28x + 21$

29) $-18x + 12$

30) $-x + 9$

31) $-18x + 12$

32) $4x - 48$

33) $12x - 2$

34) $40x + 24$

35) 6

36) 14

37) 0

38) 2

39) 53

40) 2

41) 20

42) 11

43) 31

44) 73

45) 70

46) -45

47) 42

48) 15

49) 11

50) -16

51) 22

52) 22

53) 50

CHAPTER

8 Equations and Inequalities

Math topics that you'll learn in this chapter:

- ☑ One-Step Equations
- ☑ Multi-Step Equations
- ☑ System of Equations
- ☑ Graphing Single–Variable Inequalities
- ☑ One-Step Inequalities
- ☑ Multi-Step Inequalities

One–Step Equations

- The values of two expressions on both sides of an equation are equal. Example: $ax = b$. In this equation, ax is equal to b.

- Solving an equation means finding the value of the variable.

- You only need to perform one Math operation to solve the one-step equations.

- To solve a one-step equation, find the inverse (opposite) operation is being performed.

- The inverse operations are:

  ❖ Addition and subtraction
  ❖ Multiplication and division

Examples:

Example 1. Solve this equation for x. $4x = 16, x = ?$

Solution: Here, the operation is multiplication (variable x is multiplied by 4) and its inverse operation is division. To solve this equation, divide both sides of equation by 4: $4x = 16 \rightarrow \frac{4x}{4} = \frac{16}{4} \rightarrow x = 4$

Example 2. Solve this equation. $x + 8 = 0$, $x = ?$

Solution: In this equation 8 is added to the variable x. The inverse operation of addition is subtraction. To solve this equation, subtract 8 from both sides of the equation: $x + 8 - 8 = 0 - 8$. Then: $\rightarrow x = -8$

Example 3. Solve this equation for x. $x - 12 = 0$

Solution: Here, the operation is subtraction and its inverse operation is addition. To solve this equation, add 12 to both sides of the equation:

$$x - 12 + 12 = 0 + 12 \rightarrow x = 12$$

Multi−Step Equations

- To solve a multi-step equation, combine "like" terms on one side.

- Bring variables to one side by adding or subtracting.

- Simplify using the inverse of addition or subtraction.

- Simplify further by using the inverse of multiplication or division.

- Check your solution by plugging the value of the variable into the original equation.

Examples:

Example 1. Solve this equation for x. $4x + 8 = 20 - 2x$

Solution: First, bring variables to one side by adding $2x$ to both sides. Then: $4x + 8 + 2x = 20 - 2x + 2x \to 4x + 8 + 2x = 20$.

Simplify: $6x + 8 = 20$ Now, subtract 8 from both sides of the equation:

$6x + 8 - 8 = 20 - 8 \to 6x = 12 \to$ Divide both sides by 6:

$6x = 12 \to \dfrac{6x}{6} = \dfrac{12}{6} \to x = 2$

Let's check this solution by substituting the value of 2 for x in the original equation:

$x = 2 \to 4x + 8 = 20 - 2x \to 4(2) + 8 = 20 - 2(2) \to 16 = 16$

The answer $x = 2$ is correct.

Example 2. Solve this equation for x. $-5x + 4 = 24$

Solution: Subtract 4 from both sides of the equation.

$-5x + 4 = 24 \to -5x + 4 - 4 = 24 - 4 \to -5x = 20$

Divide both sides by -5, then: $-5x = 20 \to \dfrac{-5x}{-5} = \dfrac{20}{-5} \to x = -4$

Now, check the solution:

$x = -4 \to -5x + 4 = 24 \to -5(-4) + 4 = 24 \to 24 = 24$

The answer $x = -4$ is correct.

bit.ly/3nQbSEB
Find more at

System of Equations

- A system of equations contains two equations and two variables. For example, consider the system of equations: $x - y = 1, x + y = 5$

- The easiest way to solve a system of equations is using the elimination method. The elimination method uses the addition property of equality. You can add the same value to each side of an equation.

- For the first equation above, you can add $x + y$ to the left side and 5 to the right side of the first equation: $x - y + (x + y) = 1 + 5$. Now, if you simplify, you get: $x - y + (x + y) = 1 + 5 \rightarrow 2x = 6 \rightarrow x = 3$. Now, substitute 3 for the x in the first equation: $3 - y = 1$. By solving this equation, $y = 2$

Example:

Example 1. What is the value of $x + y$ in this system of equations?

$$\begin{cases} 2x + 4y = 12 \\ 4x - 2y = -16 \end{cases}$$

Solution: Solving a System of Equations by Elimination:

Multiply the first equation by (-2), then add it to the second equation.

$$\begin{array}{r} -2(2x + 4y = 12) \\ 4x - 2y = -16 \end{array} \Rightarrow \begin{array}{r} -4x - 8y = -24 \\ 4x - 2y = -16 \end{array} \Rightarrow -10y = -40 \Rightarrow y = 4$$

Plug in the value of y into one of the equations and solve for x.

$2x + 4(4) = 12 \Rightarrow 2x + 16 = 12 \Rightarrow 2x = -4 \Rightarrow x = -2$

Thus, $x + y = -2 + 4 = 2$

Graphing Single–Variable Inequalities

- An inequality compares two expressions using an inequality sign.

- Inequality signs are: "less than" <, "greater than" >, "less than or equal to" ≤, and "greater than or equal to" ≥.

- To graph a single–variable inequality, find the value of the inequality on the number line.

- For less than (<) or greater than (>) draw an open circle on the value of the variable. If there is an equal sign too, then use a filled circle.

- Draw an arrow to the right for greater or to the left for less than.

Examples:

Example 1. Draw a graph for this inequality. $x > 2$

Solution: Since the variable is greater than 2, then we need to find 2 in the number line and draw an open circle on it. Then, draw an arrow to the right.

Example 2. Graph this inequality. $x \leq -3$.

Solution: Since the variable is less than or equal to −3, then we need to find −3 in the number line and draw a filled circle on it. Then, draw an arrow to the left.

One−Step Inequalities

- An inequality compares two expressions using an inequality sign.

- Inequality signs are: "less than" <, "greater than" >, "less than or equal to" ≤, and "greater than or equal to" ≥.

- You only need to perform one Math operation to solve the one-step inequalities.

- To solve one-step inequalities, find the inverse (opposite) operation is being performed.

- For dividing or multiplying both sides by negative numbers, flip the direction of the inequality sign.

Examples:

Example 1. Solve this inequality for x. $x + 5 \geq 4$

Solution: The inverse (opposite) operation of addition is subtraction. In this inequality, 5 is added to x. To isolate x we need to subtract 5 from both sides of the inequality.
Then: $x + 5 \geq 4 \rightarrow x + 5 - 5 \geq 4 - 5 \rightarrow x \geq -1$. The solution is: $x \geq -1$

Example 2. Solve the inequality. $x - 3 > -6$.

Solution: 3 is subtracted from x. Add 3 to both sides.
$x - 3 > -6 \rightarrow x - 3 + 3 > -6 + 3 \rightarrow x > -3$

Example 3. Solve. $4x \leq -8$.

Solution: 4 is multiplied to x. Divide both sides by 4.
Then: $4x \leq -8 \rightarrow \frac{4x}{4} \leq \frac{-8}{4} \rightarrow x \leq -2$

Example 4. Solve. $-3x \leq 6$.

Solution: -3 is multiplied to x. Divide both sides by -3. Remember when dividing or multiplying both sides of an inequality by negative numbers, flip the direction of the inequality sign.
Then: $-3x \leq 6 \rightarrow \frac{-3x}{-3} \geq \frac{6}{-3} \rightarrow x \geq -2$

Multi–Step Inequalities

- To solve a multi-step inequality, combine "like" terms on one side.

- Bring variables to one side by adding or subtracting.

- Isolate the variable.

- Simplify using the inverse of addition or subtraction.

- Simplify further by using the inverse of multiplication or division.

- For dividing or multiplying both sides by negative numbers, flip the direction of the inequality sign.

Examples:

Example 1. Solve this inequality. $8x - 2 \leq 14$

Solution: In this inequality, 2 is subtracted from $8x$. The inverse of subtraction is addition. Add 2 to both sides of the inequality:

$8x - 2 + 2 \leq 14 + 2 \rightarrow 8x \leq 16$

Now, divide both sides by 8. Then: $8x \leq 16 \rightarrow \frac{8x}{8} \leq \frac{16}{8} \rightarrow x \leq 2$

The solution of this inequality is $x \leq 2$.

Example 2. Solve this inequality. $3x + 9 < 12$

Solution: First, subtract 9 from both sides: $3x + 9 - 9 < 12 - 9$

Then simplify: $3x + 9 - 9 < 12 - 9 \rightarrow 3x < 3$

Now divide both sides by 3: $\frac{3x}{3} < \frac{3}{3} \rightarrow x < 1$

Example 3. Solve this inequality. $-5x + 3 \geq 8$

Solution: First, subtract 3 from both sides:

$-5x + 3 - 3 \geq 8 - 3 \rightarrow -5x \geq 5$

Divide both sides by -5. Remember that you need to flip the direction of inequality sign. $-5x \geq 5 \rightarrow \frac{-5x}{-5} \leq \frac{5}{-5} \rightarrow x \leq -1$

bit.ly/2WK1xOr

Find more at

Chapter 8: Practices

✍ Solve each equation. (One–Step Equations)

1) $x + 6 = 3 \rightarrow x =$ _____ --

2) $5 = 11 - x \rightarrow x =$ _____

3) $-3 = 8 + x \rightarrow x =$ _____

4) $x - 2 = -7 \rightarrow x =$ _____

5) $-15 = x + 6 \rightarrow x =$ _____

6) $10 - x = -2 \rightarrow x =$ _____

7) $22 - x = -9 \rightarrow x =$ _____

8) $-4 + x = 28 \rightarrow x =$ _____

9) $11 - x = -7 \rightarrow x =$ _____

10) $35 - x = -7 \rightarrow x =$ _____

✍ Solve each equation. (Multi–Step Equations)

11) $4(x + 2) = 12 \rightarrow x =$ _____

12) $-6(6 - x) = 12 \rightarrow x =$ _____

13) $5 = -5(x + 2) \rightarrow x =$ _____

14) $-10 = 2(4 + x) \rightarrow x =$ _____

15) $4(x + 2) = -12, x =$ _____

16) $-6(3 + 2x) = 30, x =$ _____

17) $-3(4 - x) = 12, x =$ _____

18) $-4(6 - x) = 16, x =$ _____

✍ Solve each system of equations.

19) $\begin{cases} x + 6y = 32 \\ x + 3y = 17 \end{cases}$ $x =$ _____ $y =$ _____

20) $\begin{cases} 3x + y = 15 \\ x + 2y = 10 \end{cases}$ $x =$ _____ $y =$ _____

21) $\begin{cases} 3x + 5y = 17 \\ 2x + y = 9 \end{cases}$ $x =$ _____ $y =$ _____

22) $\begin{cases} 5x - 2y = -8 \\ -6x + 2y = 10 \end{cases}$ $x =$ _____ $y =$ _____

Effortless
Math
Education

✎ **Draw a graph for each inequality.**

23) $x \leq -3$ ← | -6 | -5 | -4 | -3 | -2 | -1 | 0 | 1 | 2 | 3 | 4 | 5 | 6 | →

24) $x > -5$ ← | -6 | -5 | -4 | -3 | -2 | -1 | 0 | 1 | 2 | 3 | 4 | 5 | 6 | →

✎ **Solve each inequality and graph it.**

25) $x - 2 \geq -2$ ← | -6 | -5 | -4 | -3 | -2 | -1 | 0 | 1 | 2 | 3 | 4 | 5 | 6 | →

26) $2x - 3 < 9$ ← | -6 | -5 | -4 | -3 | -2 | -1 | 0 | 1 | 2 | 3 | 4 | 5 | 6 | →

✎ **Solve each inequality.**

27) $x + 13 > 4$

28) $x + 6 > 5$

29) $-12 + 2x \leq 26$

30) $-2 + 8x \leq 14$

31) $6 + 4x \leq 18$

32) $4(x + 3) \geq -12$

33) $2(6 + x) \geq -12$

34) $3(x - 5) < -6$

35) $10 + 5x < -15$

36) $6(6 + x) \geq -18$

37) $2(x - 5) \geq -14$

38) $6(x + 4) < -12$

39) $3(x - 8) \geq -48$

40) $-(6 - 4x) > -30$

41) $2(2 + 2x) > -60$

42) $-3(4 + 2x) > -24$

Effortless
Math
Education

Chapter 8: Answers

1) -3

2) 6

3) -11

4) -5

5) -21

6) 12

7) 31

8) 32

9) 18

10) 42

11) 1

12) 8

13) -3

14) -9

15) -5

16) -4

17) 8

18) 10

19) $x = 2, y = 5$

20) $x = 4, y = 3$

21) $x = 4, y = 1$

22) $x = -2, y = -1$

23) $x \le -3$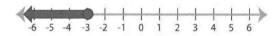

24) $x > -5$

25) $x \ge 0$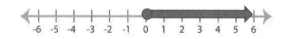

26) $x < 6$

27) $x > -9$

28) $x > -1$

29) $x \le 19$

30) $x \le 2$

31) $x \le 3$

32) $x \ge -6$

33) $x \ge -12$

34) $x < 3$

35) $x < -5$

36) $x \ge -9$

37) $x \ge -2$

38) $x < -6$

39) $x \ge -8$

40) $x > -6$

41) $x > -16$

42) $x < 2$

9 Geometry and Solid Figures

Math topics that you'll learn in this chapter:

- ☑ The Pythagorean Theorem
- ☑ Triangles
- ☑ Polygons
- ☑ Circles
- ☑ Trapezoids
- ☑ Cubes
- ☑ Rectangle Prisms
- ☑ Cylinder

The Pythagorean Theorem

- You can use the Pythagorean Theorem to find a missing side in a right triangle.

- In any right triangle: $a^2 + b^2 = c^2$

Examples:

Example 4. Right triangle ABC (not shown) has two legs of lengths 3 cm (AB) and 4 cm (AC). What is the length of the hypotenuse of the triangle (side BC)?

Solution: Use Pythagorean Theorem: $a^2 + b^2 = c^2$, $a = 3$, and $b = 4$
Then: $a^2 + b^2 = c^2 \rightarrow 3^2 + 4^2 = c^2 \rightarrow 9 + 16 = c^2 \rightarrow 25 = c^2 \rightarrow c = \sqrt{25} = 5$
The length of the hypotenuse is 5 cm.

Example 5. Find the hypotenuse of this triangle.

Solution: Use Pythagorean Theorem: $a^2 + b^2 = c^2$
Then: $a^2 + b^2 = c^2 \rightarrow 8^2 + 6^2 = c^2 \rightarrow 64 + 36 = c^2$
$c^2 = 100 \rightarrow c = \sqrt{100} = 10$

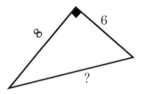

Example 6. Find the length of the missing side in this triangle.

Solution: Use Pythagorean Theorem: $a^2 + b^2 = c^2$
Then: $a^2 + b^2 = c^2 \rightarrow 12^2 + b^2 = 15^2 \rightarrow 144 + b^2 = 225 \rightarrow$
$\quad\quad\quad b^2 = 225 - 144 \rightarrow b^2 = 81 \rightarrow b = \sqrt{81} = 9$

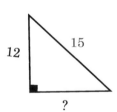

Triangles

- In any triangle, the sum of all angles is 180 degrees.

- Area of a triangle $= \frac{1}{2}(base \times height)$

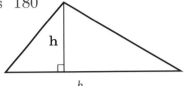

Examples:

What is the area of the following triangles?

Example 1.

Solution: Use the area formula:

Area $= \frac{1}{2}(base \times height)$

$base = 14$ and $height = 10$

Area $= \frac{1}{2}(14 \times 10) = \frac{1}{2}(140) = 70$

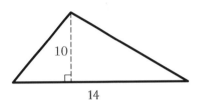

Example 2.

Solution: Use the area formula:

Area $= \frac{1}{2}(base \times height)$

$base = 16$ and $height = 8$; Area $= \frac{1}{2}(16 \times 8) = \frac{128}{2} = 64$

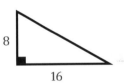

Example 3. What is the missing angle in this triangle?

Solution:

In any triangle, the sum of all angles is 180 degrees.

Let x be the missing angle.

Then: $55 + 80 + x = 180$;

$\rightarrow 135 + x = 180 \rightarrow x = 180 - 135 = 45$

The missing angle is 45 degrees.

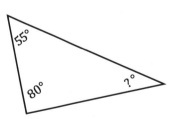

Polygons

- The perimeter of a square = $4 \times side = 4s$

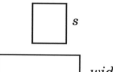

- The perimeter of a rectangle= $2(width + length)$

- The perimeter of trapezoid= $a + b + c + d$

- The perimeter of a regular hexagon = $6a$

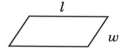

- The perimeter of a parallelogram = $2(l + w)$

Examples:

Example 1. Find the perimeter of following regular hexagon.

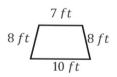

Solution: Since the hexagon is regular, all sides are equal.
Then: The perimeter of The hexagon = $6 \times (one\ side)$
The perimeter of The hexagon = $6 \times (one\ side) = 6 \times 8 = 48\ m$

Example 2. Find the perimeter of following trapezoid.

Solution: The perimeter of a trapezoid = $a + b + c + d$
The perimeter of the trapezoid = $7 + 8 + 8 + 10 = 33\ ft$

Circles

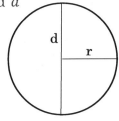

- In a circle, variable r is usually used for the radius and d for diameter.

- *Area of a circle* $= \pi r^2$ (π is about 3.14)

- *Circumference of a circle* $= 2\pi r$

Examples:

Example 1. Find the area of this circle.

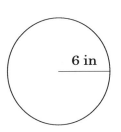

Solution:

Use area formula: $Area = \pi r^2$

$r = 6\ in \rightarrow Area = \pi(6)^2 = 36\pi$, $\pi = 3.14$

Then: $Area = 36 \times 3.14 = 113.04\ in^2$

Example 2. Find the Circumference of this circle.

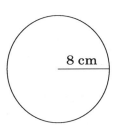

Solution:

Use Circumference formula: $Circumference = 2\pi r$

$r = 8\ cm \rightarrow Circumference = 2\pi(8) = 16\pi$

$\pi = 3.14$ Then: $Circumference = 16 \times 3.14 = 50.24\ cm$

Example 3. Find the area of the circle.

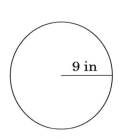

Solution:

Use area formula: $Area = \pi r^2$,

$r = 9\ in$ then: $Area = \pi(9)^2 = 81\pi$, $\pi = 3.14$

Then: $Area = 81 \times 3.14 = 254.34\ in^2$

bit.ly/3nJdOP2

Find more at

Trapezoids

- A quadrilateral with at least one pair of parallel sides is a trapezoid.

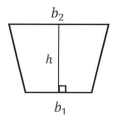

- Area of a trapezoid $= \frac{1}{2}h(b_1 + b_2)$

Examples:

Example 1. Calculate the area of this trapezoid.

Solution:

Use area formula: $A = \frac{1}{2}h(b_1 + b_2)$

$b_1 = 6\ cm$, $b_2 = 10\ cm$ and $h = 12\ cm$

Then: $A = \frac{1}{2}(12)(10 + 6) = 6(16) = 96\ cm^2$

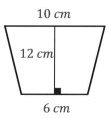

Example 2. Calculate the area of this trapezoid.

Solution:

Use area formula: $A = \frac{1}{2}h(b_1 + b_2)$

$b_1 = 10\ cm$, $b_2 = 18\ cm$ and $h = 14\ cm$

Then: $A = \frac{1}{2}(14)(10 + 18) = 7(28) = 196\ cm^2$

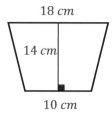

Cubes

- A cube is a three-dimensional solid object bounded by six square sides.

- Volume is the measure of the amount of space inside of a solid figure, like a cube, ball, cylinder or pyramid.

- The volume of a cube = $(one\ side)^3$

- The surface area of a cube = $6 \times (one\ side)^2$

Examples:

Example 1. Find the volume and surface area of this cube.

Solution: Use volume formula: $volume = (one\ side)^3$
Then: $volume = (one\ side)^3 = (3)^3 = 27\ cm^3$
Use surface area formula:
surface area of cube: $6(one\ side)^2 = 6(3)^2 = 6(9) = 54\ cm^2$

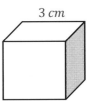

3 cm

Example 2. Find the volume and surface area of this cube.

Solution: Use volume formula: $volume = (one\ side)^3$
Then: $volume = (one\ side)^3 = (6)^3 = 216\ cm^3$
Use surface area formula:
surface area of cube: $6(one\ side)^2 = 6(6)^2 = 6(36) = 216\ cm^2$

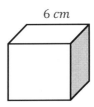

6 cm

Example 3. Find the volume and surface area of this cube.

Solution: Use volume formula: $volume = (one\ side)^3$
Then: $volume = (one\ side)^3 = (8)^3 = 512\ m^3$
Use surface area formula:
surface area of cube: $6(one\ side)^2 = 6(8)^2 = 6(64) = 384\ m^2$

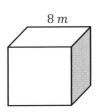

8 m

bit.ly/2M6PfOl

Find more at

Rectangular Prisms

- A rectangular prism is a solid 3-dimensional object with six rectangular faces.

- The volume of a Rectangular prism $= Length \times Width \times Height$

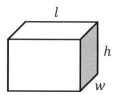

$Volume = l \times w \times h$

$Surface\ area = 2 \times (wh + lw + lh)$

Examples:

Example 1. Find the volume and surface area of this rectangular prism.

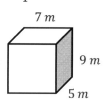

Solution: Use volume formula: $Volume = l \times w \times h$

Then: $Volume = 7 \times 5 \times 9 = 315\ m^3$

Use surface area formula: $Surface\ area = 2 \times (wh + lw + lh)$

Then: $Surface\ area = 2 \times \big((5 \times 9) + (7 \times 5) + (7 \times 9)\big)$

$\qquad\qquad = 2 \times (45 + 35 + 63) = 2 \times (143) = 286\ m^2$

Example 2. Find the volume and surface area of this rectangular prism.

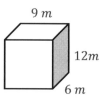

Solution: Use volume formula: $Volume = l \times w \times h$

Then: $Volume = 9 \times 6 \times 12 = 648\ m^3$

Use surface area formula: $Surface\ area = 2 \times (wh + lw + lh)$

Then: $Surface\ area = 2 \times \big((6 \times 12) + (9 \times 6) + (9 \times 12)\big)$

$\qquad\qquad = 2 \times (72 + 54 + 108) = 2 \times (234) = 468\ m^2$

Cylinder

- A cylinder is a solid geometric figure with straight parallel sides and a circular or oval cross-section.

- *Volume of a Cylinder = $\pi(radius)^2 \times height$, $\pi \approx 3.14$*

- *Surface area of a cylinder = $2\pi r^2 + 2\pi rh$*

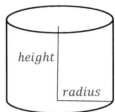

Examples:

Example 1. Find the volume and Surface area of the follow Cylinder.

Solution: Use volume formula:

$Volume = \pi(radius)^2 \times height$

Then: $Volume = \pi(4)^2 \times 10 = 16\pi \times 10 = 160\pi$

$\pi = 3.14$ then: $Volume = 160\pi = 160 \times 3.14 = 502.4\ cm^3$

Use surface area formula: $Surface\ area = 2\pi r^2 + 2\pi rh$

Then: $2\pi(4)^2 + 2\pi(4)(10) = 2\pi(16) + 2\pi(40) = 32\pi + 80\pi = 112\pi$

$\pi = 3.14$ Then: $Surface\ area = 112 \times 3.14 = 351.68\ cm^2$

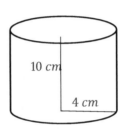

Example 2. Find the volume and Surface area of the follow Cylinder.

Solution: Use volume formula:

$Volume = \pi(radius)^2 \times height$

Then: $Volume = \pi(5)^2 \times 8 = \pi 25 \times 8 = 200\pi$

$\pi = 3.14$ then: $Volume = 200\pi = 628\ cm^3$

Use surface area formula: $Surface\ area = 2\pi r^2 + 2\pi rh$

Then: $= 2\pi(5)^2 + 2\pi(5)(8) = 2\pi(25) + 2\pi(40) = 50\pi + 80\pi = 130\pi$

$\pi = 3.14$ then: $Surface\ area = 130 \times 3.14 = 408.2\ cm^2$

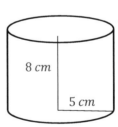

bit.ly/37LtcVM
Find more at

Chapter 9: Practices

✍ Find the missing side?

1)   2)   3)   4)

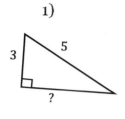   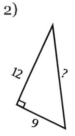   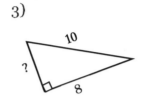   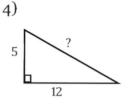

✍ Find the measure of the unknown angle in each triangle.

5)   6)   7)   8)

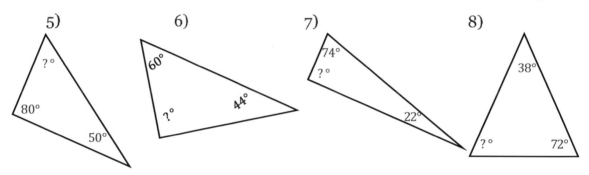

✍ Find the area of each triangle.

9)   10)   11)   12)

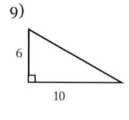 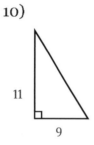 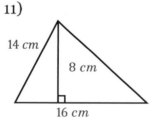 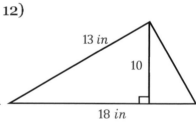

✍ Find the perimeter or circumference of each shape.

13)   14)   15)   16) *regular hexagon*

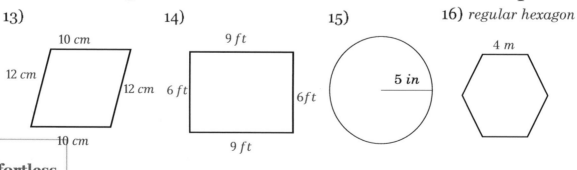

✍ **Find the area of each trapezoid.**

17)   18)   19)   20)

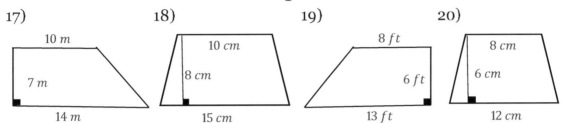

✍ **Find the volume of each cube.**

21)   22)   23)   24)

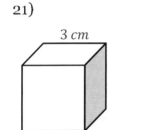 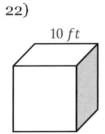 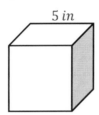 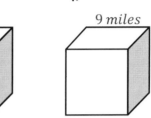

✍ **Find the volume of each Rectangular Prism.**

25)   26)   27)

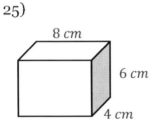 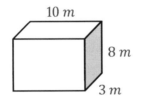 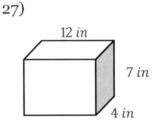

✍ **Find the volume of each Cylinder. Round your answer to the nearest tenth. ($\pi = 3.14$)**

28)   29)   30)

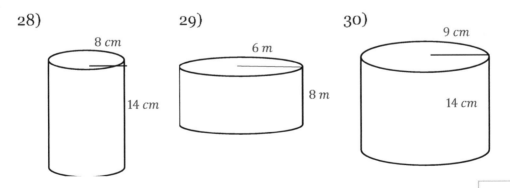

Effortless
Math
Education

Chapter 9: Answers

1) 4	11) $64\ cm^2$	21) $27\ cm^3$
2) 15	12) $90\ in^2$	22) $1,000\ ft^3$
3) 6	13) $44\ cm$	23) $125\ in^3$
4) 13	14) $30\ ft$	24) $729\ mi^3$
5) 50	15) $10\ \pi \approx 31.4\ in$	25) $192\ cm^3$
6) 76	16) $24\ m$	26) $240\ m^3$
7) 84	17) $84\ m^2$	27) $336\ in^3$
8) 70	18) $100\ cm^2$	28) $2,813.44\ cm^3$
9) 30	19) $63\ ft^2$	29) $904.32\ m^3$
10) 49.5	20) $60\ cm^2$	30) $3,560.76\ cm^3$

CHAPTER

10 Statistics

Math topics that you'll learn in this chapter:

- ☑ Mean, Median, Mode, and Range of the Given Data
- ☑ Pie Graph
- ☑ Probability Problems
- ☑ Permutations and Combinations

Mean, Median, Mode, and Range of the Given Data

- Mean: $\dfrac{sum\ of\ the\ data}{total\ number\ of\ data\ entires}$

- Mode: the value in the list that appears most often

- Median: is the middle number of a group of numbers arranged in order by size.

- Range: the difference of the largest value and smallest value in the list

Examples:

Example 1. What is the mode of these numbers? $5, 6, 8, 6, 8, 5, 3, 5$

Solution: Mode: the value in the list that appears most often.
Therefore, the mode is number 5. There are three number 5 in the data.

Example 2. What is the median of these numbers? $6, 11, 15, 10, 17, 20, 7$

Solution: Write the numbers in order: $6, 7, 10, 11, 15, 17, 20$
The median is the number in the middle. Therefore, the median is 11.

Example 3. What is the mean of these numbers? $7, 2, 3, 2, 4, 8, 7, 5$

Solution: Mean: $\dfrac{sum\ of\ the\ data}{total\ number\ of\ data\ entires} = \dfrac{7+2+3+2+4+8+7+5}{8} = \dfrac{38}{8} = 4.75$

Example 4. What is the range in this list? $3, 7, 12, 6, 15, 20, 8$

Solution: Range is the difference of the largest value and smallest value in the list. The largest value is 20 and the smallest value is 3.
Then: $20 - 3 = 17$

Pie Graph

- A Pie Chart is a circle chart divided into sectors, each sector represents the relative size of each value.

- Pie charts represent a snapshot of how a group is broken down into smaller pieces.

Example:

A library has 750 books that include Mathematics, Physics, Chemistry, English and History. Use the following graph to answer the questions.

Example 1. What is the number of Mathematics books?

Solution: Number of total books = 750

Percent of Mathematics books = 28% = 0.28

Then, the number of Mathematics books: $0.28 \times 750 = 210$

Example 2. What is the number of History books?

Solution: Number of total books = 750

Percent of History books = 12% = 0.12

Then: $0.12 \times 750 = 90$

Example 3. What is the number of Chemistry books?

Solution: Number of total books = 750

Percent of Chemistry books = 22% = 0.22

Then: $0.22 \times 750 = 165$

Probability Problems

- Probability is the likelihood of something happening in the future. It is expressed as a number between zero (can never happen) to 1 (will always happen).

- Probability can be expressed as a fraction, a decimal, or a percent.

- Probability formula: $Probability = \dfrac{number\ of\ desired\ outcomes}{number\ of\ total\ outcomes}$

Examples:

Example 1. Anita's trick–or–treat bag contains 10 pieces of chocolate, 16 suckers, 16 pieces of gum, 22 pieces of licorice. If she randomly pulls a piece of candy from her bag, what is the probability of her pulling out a piece of sucker?

Solution: $Probability = \dfrac{number\ of\ desired\ outcomes}{number\ of\ total\ outcomes}$

Probability of pulling out a piece of sucker $= \dfrac{16}{10 + 16 + 16 + 22} = \dfrac{16}{64} = \dfrac{1}{4}$

Example 2. A bag contains 20 balls: four green, five black, eight blue, a brown, a red and one white. If 19 balls are removed from the bag at random, what is the probability that a brown ball has been removed?

Solution: If 19 balls are removed from the bag at random, there will be one ball in the bag. The probability of choosing a brown ball is 1 out of 20. Therefore, the probability of not choosing a brown ball is 19 out of 20 and the probability of having not a brown ball after removing 19 balls is the same. The answer is: $\dfrac{19}{20}$

Permutations and Combinations

Factorials are products, indicated by an exclamation mark. For example, $4! = 4 \times 3 \times 2 \times 1$ (Remember that $0!$ is defined to be equal to 1)

- **Permutations:** The number of ways to choose a sample of k elements from a set of n distinct objects where order does matter, and replacements are not allowed. For a permutation problem, use this formula:

$$_n\text{P}_k = \frac{n!}{(n-k)!}$$

- **Combination:** The number of ways to choose a sample of r elements from a set of n distinct objects where order does not matter, and replacements are not allowed. For a combination problem, use this formula:

$$_n\text{C}_r = \frac{n!}{r!\,(n-r)!}$$

Examples:

Example 1. How many ways can the first and second place be awarded to 7 people?

Solution: Since the order matters, (the first and second place are different!) we need to use permutation formula where n is 7 and k is 2. Then: $\frac{n!}{(n-k)!} = \frac{7!}{(7-2)!} = \frac{7!}{5!} = \frac{7 \times 6 \times 5!}{5!}$, remove $5!$ from both sides of the fraction. Then: $\frac{7 \times 6 \times 5!}{5!} = 7 \times 6 = 42$

Example 2. How many ways can we pick a team of 3 people from a group of 8?

Solution: Since the order doesn't matter, we need to use a combination formula where n is 8 and r is 3.
Then: $\frac{n!}{r!\,(n-r)!} = \frac{8!}{3!\,(8-3)!} = \frac{8!}{3!\,(5)!} = \frac{8 \times 7 \times 6 \times 5!}{3!\,(5)!} = \frac{8 \times 7 \times 6}{3 \times 2 \times 1} = \frac{336}{6} = 56$

bit.ly/34BQgUY

Find more at

Chapter 10: Practices

✎ Find the values of the Given Data.

1) 6, 11, 5, 3, 6

Mode: _____   Range: _____

Mean: _____   Median: _____

2) 4, 9, 1, 9, 6, 7

Mode: _____   Range: _____

Mean: _____   Median: _____

3) 10, 3, 6, 10, 4, 15

Mode: _____   Range: _____

Mean: _____   Median: _____

4) 12, 4, 8, 9, 3, 12, 15

Mode: _____   Range: _____

Mean: _____   Median: _____

✎ The circle graph below shows all Bob's expenses for last month. Bob spent $790 on his Rent last month.

5) How much did Bob's total expenses last month? _____

6) How much did Bob spend for foods last month? _____

7) How much did Bob spend for his bills last month? _____

8) How much did Bob spend on his car last month? _____

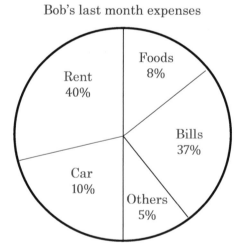

Bob's last month expenses

Rent 40%
Foods 8%
Bills 37%
Others 5%
Car 10%

✏ Solve.

9) Bag A contains 8 red marbles and 6 green marbles. Bag B contains 5 black marbles and 7 orange marbles. What is the probability of selecting a green marble at random from bag A? What is the probability of selecting a black marble at random from Bag B?

_____   _____

✏ Solve.

10) Susan is baking cookies. She uses sugar, flour, butter, and eggs. How many different orders of ingredients can she try? _____

11) Jason is planning for his vacation. He wants to go to museum, go to the beach, and play volleyball. How many different ways of ordering are there for him? _____

12) In how many ways can a team of 6 basketball players choose a captain and co-captain? _____

13) How many ways can you give 5 balls to your 8 friends? _____

14) A professor is going to arrange her 5 students in a straight line. In how many ways can she do this? _____

15) In how many ways can a teacher chooses 12 out of 15 students?

_____

Effortless
Math
Education

Chapter 10: Answers

1) Mode: 6, Range: 8, Mean: 6.2, Median: 6

2) Mode: 9, Range:8, Mean: 6, Median: 6.5

3) Mode: 10, Range: 12, Mean: 8, Median: 8

4) Mode: 12, Range: 12, Mean: 9, Median: 9

5) $1,975

6) $158

7) $730.75

8) $197.50

9) $\frac{3}{7}, \frac{5}{12}$

10) 24

11) 6

12) 30 (it's a permutation problem)

13) 56 (it's a combination problem)

14) 120

15) 455 (it's a combination problem)

Time to Test

Time to refine your skill with a practice examination

Take a practice ISEE Middle Level Mathematics Test to simulate the test day experience. After you've finished, score your test using the answer keys.

Before You Start

- You'll need a pencil and a timer to take the test.
- After you've finished the test, review the answer key to see where you went wrong.
- Use the answer sheet provided to record your answers. (You can cut it out or photocopy it)
- Students receive 1 point for every correct answer. There is no penalty for wrong or skipped questions.

Calculators are NOT permitted for the ISEE Middle Level Test

Good Luck!

ISEE Middle Level Math Practice Test 1

2022 - 2023

Two Parts

Total number of questions: 84

Part 1 (Quantitative Reasoning): 37 questions

Part 2 (Mathematics Achievement): 47 questions

Total time for two parts: 75 Minutes

ISEE Middle Level Practice Test Answer Sheets

Remove (or photocopy) this answer sheet and use it to complete the practice test.

ISEE Middle Level Practice Test 1

Quantitative Reasoning

1. Ⓐ Ⓑ Ⓒ Ⓓ
2. Ⓐ Ⓑ Ⓒ Ⓓ
3. Ⓐ Ⓑ Ⓒ Ⓓ
4. Ⓐ Ⓑ Ⓒ Ⓓ
5. Ⓐ Ⓑ Ⓒ Ⓓ
6. Ⓐ Ⓑ Ⓒ Ⓓ
7. Ⓐ Ⓑ Ⓒ Ⓓ
8. Ⓐ Ⓑ Ⓒ Ⓓ
9. Ⓐ Ⓑ Ⓒ Ⓓ
10. Ⓐ Ⓑ Ⓒ Ⓓ
11. Ⓐ Ⓑ Ⓒ Ⓓ
12. Ⓐ Ⓑ Ⓒ Ⓓ
13. Ⓐ Ⓑ Ⓒ Ⓓ
14. Ⓐ Ⓑ Ⓒ Ⓓ
15. Ⓐ Ⓑ Ⓒ Ⓓ
16. Ⓐ Ⓑ Ⓒ Ⓓ
17. Ⓐ Ⓑ Ⓒ Ⓓ
18. Ⓐ Ⓑ Ⓒ Ⓓ
19. Ⓐ Ⓑ Ⓒ Ⓓ
20. Ⓐ Ⓑ Ⓒ Ⓓ
21. Ⓐ Ⓑ Ⓒ Ⓓ
22. Ⓐ Ⓑ Ⓒ Ⓓ
23. Ⓐ Ⓑ Ⓒ Ⓓ
24. Ⓐ Ⓑ Ⓒ Ⓓ

25. Ⓐ Ⓑ Ⓒ Ⓓ
26. Ⓐ Ⓑ Ⓒ Ⓓ
27. Ⓐ Ⓑ Ⓒ Ⓓ
28. Ⓐ Ⓑ Ⓒ Ⓓ
29. Ⓐ Ⓑ Ⓒ Ⓓ
30. Ⓐ Ⓑ Ⓒ Ⓓ
31. Ⓐ Ⓑ Ⓒ Ⓓ
32. Ⓐ Ⓑ Ⓒ Ⓓ
33. Ⓐ Ⓑ Ⓒ Ⓓ
34. Ⓐ Ⓑ Ⓒ Ⓓ
35. Ⓐ Ⓑ Ⓒ Ⓓ
36. Ⓐ Ⓑ Ⓒ Ⓓ
37. Ⓐ Ⓑ Ⓒ Ⓓ

Mathematics Achievement

1. Ⓐ Ⓑ Ⓒ Ⓓ
2. Ⓐ Ⓑ Ⓒ Ⓓ
3. Ⓐ Ⓑ Ⓒ Ⓓ
4. Ⓐ Ⓑ Ⓒ Ⓓ
5. Ⓐ Ⓑ Ⓒ Ⓓ
6. Ⓐ Ⓑ Ⓒ Ⓓ
7. Ⓐ Ⓑ Ⓒ Ⓓ
8. Ⓐ Ⓑ Ⓒ Ⓓ
9. Ⓐ Ⓑ Ⓒ Ⓓ
10. Ⓐ Ⓑ Ⓒ Ⓓ
11. Ⓐ Ⓑ Ⓒ Ⓓ
12. Ⓐ Ⓑ Ⓒ Ⓓ
13. Ⓐ Ⓑ Ⓒ Ⓓ
14. Ⓐ Ⓑ Ⓒ Ⓓ
15. Ⓐ Ⓑ Ⓒ Ⓓ
16. Ⓐ Ⓑ Ⓒ Ⓓ
17. Ⓐ Ⓑ Ⓒ Ⓓ
18. Ⓐ Ⓑ Ⓒ Ⓓ
19. Ⓐ Ⓑ Ⓒ Ⓓ
20. Ⓐ Ⓑ Ⓒ Ⓓ
21. Ⓐ Ⓑ Ⓒ Ⓓ
22. Ⓐ Ⓑ Ⓒ Ⓓ
23. Ⓐ Ⓑ Ⓒ Ⓓ
24. Ⓐ Ⓑ Ⓒ Ⓓ

25. Ⓐ Ⓑ Ⓒ Ⓓ
26. Ⓐ Ⓑ Ⓒ Ⓓ
27. Ⓐ Ⓑ Ⓒ Ⓓ
28. Ⓐ Ⓑ Ⓒ Ⓓ
29. Ⓐ Ⓑ Ⓒ Ⓓ
30. Ⓐ Ⓑ Ⓒ Ⓓ
31. Ⓐ Ⓑ Ⓒ Ⓓ
32. Ⓐ Ⓑ Ⓒ Ⓓ
33. Ⓐ Ⓑ Ⓒ Ⓓ
34. Ⓐ Ⓑ Ⓒ Ⓓ
35. Ⓐ Ⓑ Ⓒ Ⓓ
36. Ⓐ Ⓑ Ⓒ Ⓓ
37. Ⓐ Ⓑ Ⓒ Ⓓ
38. Ⓐ Ⓑ Ⓒ Ⓓ
39. Ⓐ Ⓑ Ⓒ Ⓓ
40. Ⓐ Ⓑ Ⓒ Ⓓ
41. Ⓐ Ⓑ Ⓒ Ⓓ
42. Ⓐ Ⓑ Ⓒ Ⓓ
43. Ⓐ Ⓑ Ⓒ Ⓓ
44. Ⓐ Ⓑ Ⓒ Ⓓ
45. Ⓐ Ⓑ Ⓒ Ⓓ
46. Ⓐ Ⓑ Ⓒ Ⓓ
47. Ⓐ Ⓑ Ⓒ Ⓓ

ISEE Middle Level Math
Practice Test 1

Section 1

37 questions

Total time for this section: 35 Minutes

You may NOT use a calculator for this test.

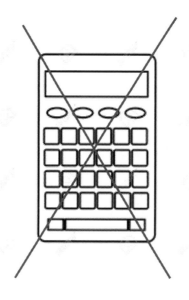

1) Solve. $\dfrac{-50 \times 0.5}{5}$

A. -16

B. -5

C. 5

D. 16

2) A \$41 shirt now selling for \$29 is discounted by what percent?

A. 20%

B. 29%

C. 40%

D. 50%

3) $562,357,741 \times 0.0001$?

A. 562,357.741

B. 56,235.7741

C. 5,623.57741

D. 562.357741

4) Jim purchased a table for 30% off and saved \$24. What was the original price of the table?

A. \$80

B. \$110

C. \$115

D. 150

5) If $f = 3x - 2y$ and $g = x + 5y$, what is $3f + g$?

A. $5x - y$

B. $5x - 2y$

C. $10x - 2y$

D. $10x - y$

6) Which of the following shows the numbers in increasing order?

A. $\frac{1}{7}, \frac{3}{5}, \frac{1}{3}, \frac{3}{4}$

B. $\frac{1}{7}, \frac{3}{5}, \frac{3}{4}, \frac{1}{3}$

C. $\frac{1}{7}, \frac{1}{3}, \frac{3}{5}, \frac{3}{4}$

D. $\frac{1}{7}, \frac{3}{4}, \frac{1}{3}, \frac{3}{5}$

7) What is the value of x in the following equation? $8^x = 512$

A. 2

B. 3

C. 4

D. 5

8) What is the value of x in the following figure?

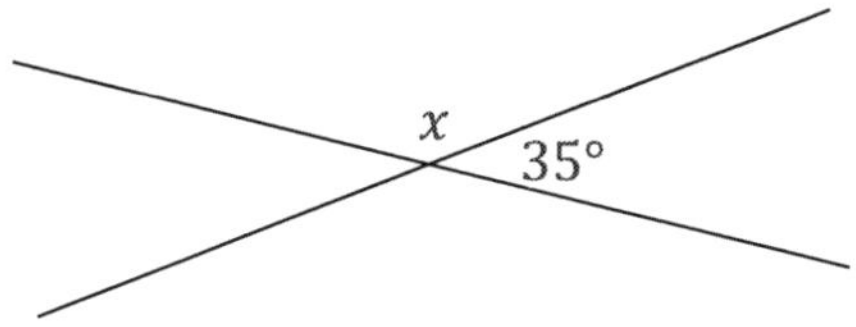

A. 35°

B. 75°

C. 115°

D. 145°

9) The score of Emma was half as that of Ava and the score of Mia was twice that of Ava. If the score of Mia was 40, what is the score of Emma?

A. 10

B. 18

C. 20

D. 30

10) The area of a circle is 49π. What is the circumference of the circle?

A. 8π

B. 14π

C. 32π

D. 49π

11) Two third of 15 is equal to $\frac{5}{2}$ of what number?

A. 25

B. 15

C. 10

D. 4

12) What is round off the result of 1.15×8.2 to the nearest tenth?

A. 6

B. 7

C. 8.06

D. 9.4

13) The perimeter of the trapezoid below (not drawn to scale) is 56. What is its area?

A. 255 cm^2

B. 234 cm^2

C. 192 cm^2

D. 180 cm^2

14) In five successive hours, a car traveled 42 km, 46 km, 52 km, 35 km and 58 km. In the next five hours, it traveled with an average speed of 60 $km\ per\ hour$. Find the total distance the car traveled in 10 hours.

A. 435 km

B. 450 km

C. 475 km

D. 533 km

15) What is the mean in the following set of numbers?

$$10, 13, 29, 37, 46, 66, 100, 124$$

A. 46.2

B. 40.5

C. 51.4

D. 53.12

16) Find $\frac{1}{2}$ of $\frac{2}{5}$ of 145?

A. 30

B. 29

C. 18

D. 4

17) The price of a laptop is decreased by 20% to $320. What is its original price?

A. $320

B. $380

C. $400

D. $455

18) A company pays its employee $7,500 plus 3% of all sales profit. If x is all sold profit, which of the following represents the employee's revenue?

A. $0.03x$

B. $0.97x - 7,500$

C. $0.03x + 7,500$

D. $0.97x + 7,500$

19) The ratio of boys and girls in a class is 7 : 4. If there are 44 students in the class, how many more girls should be enrolled to make the ratio 1 : 1?

A. 8

B. 10

C. 12

D. 16

20) Which of the following is a correct statement?

A. $\frac{3}{5} > 0.8$

B. $12\% = \frac{2}{5}$

C. $3 < \frac{5}{2}$

D. $\frac{7}{6} > 0.8$

21) What is the value of x in the following equation?

$$6(x + 1) = 4(x - 4) + 20$$

A. 12

B. -12

C. 1

D. -1

22) What is the value of x in the following figure?

A. 160

B. 145

C. 125

D. 105

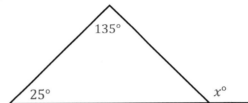

23) Car A use 4-liter petrol per 140 kilometers; car B use 3-liter petrol per 140 kilometers. If both cars drive 350 kilometers, how much more petrol does car A use?

A. 2.5

B. 10

C. 15.5

D. 25

24) What is the area of a square whose diagonal is 6?

A. 18

B. 32

C. 46

D. 64

25) What is value of $-25 - (-66)$?

A. 41

B. -91

C. -41

D. 91

Quantitative Comparisons

Direction: Questions 26 to 37 are Quantitative Comparisons Questions. Using the information provided in each question, compare the quantity in column A to the quantity in Column B. Choose on your answer sheet grid

A   if the quantity in Column A is greater

B   if the quantity in Column B is greater

C   if the two quantities are equal

D   if the relationship cannot be determined from the information given

26)

Column A	Column B
$\sqrt{36} + \sqrt{36}$	$\sqrt{72}$

27) $y = -4x - 8$

Column A	Column B
The value of x when $y = 12$	-4

28)

Column A	Column B
$6 + 4 \times 7 + 8$	$4 + 6 \times 7 - 8$

29) The average age of Joe, Michelle, and Nicole is 32.

Column A	Column B
The average age of Joe and Michelle	The average age of Michelle and Nicole

30)

Column A	Column B
$\sqrt{121 - 64}$	$\sqrt{121} - \sqrt{64}$

31) A right cylinder with radius 2 inches has volume 50π cubic inches.

Column A	Column B
The height of the cylinder	10 inches

32) x is an integer.

Column A	Column B
$\dfrac{x^6}{6}$	$\left(\dfrac{x}{6}\right)^6$

33) x is an integer greater than zero.

Column A	Column B
$\dfrac{1}{x} + x$	8

34) $\dfrac{4}{5} < x < \dfrac{6}{7}$

Column A	Column B
x	$\dfrac{5}{6}$

35) a and b are real numbers.

$$a < b$$

Column A	Column B
$|a - b|$	$|b - a|$

36) $2x^3 + 10 = 64$

$120 - 18y = 84$

Column A	Column B
x	y

37) The average of 3, 4, and x is 3.

Column A	Column B
x	average of $x, x - 6, x + 4, 2x$

ISEE Middle Level Math
Practice Test 1

Section 2

47 questions

Total time for this section: 40 Minutes

You may NOT use a calculator for this test.

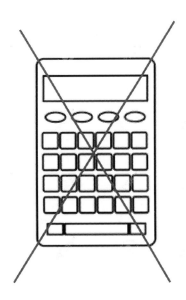

1) What number is 5 less than 50% of 46?

A. 10

B. 13

C. 18

D. 23

2) $4\left(\frac{1}{3}-\frac{1}{6}\right)+5$?

A. 4

B. 4.5

C. 5.66 …

D. 5

3) What number is 15 more than 20% of 120?

A. 39

B. 29

C. 25

D. 20

4) In a bundle of 85 pencils, 42 are red and the rest are blue. About what percent of the bundle is composed of blue pencils?

A. 62%

B. 58%

C. 54%

D. 51%

5) What is the value of x in the following equation?

$$(x+6)^3 = 64$$

A. 1

B. −1

C. 2

D. −2

6) If a box contains red and blue balls in ratio of $3:2$, how many red balls are there if 90 blue balls are in the box?

A. 140

B. 135

C. 60

D. 10

7) What is the difference in perimeter between a 8 cm by 5 cm rectangle and a circle with diameter of 12 cm? ($\pi = 3$)

A. 8 cm

B. 9 cm

C. 10 cm

D. 11 cm

8) When a number is subtracted from 27 and the difference is divided by that number, the result is 2. What is the value of the number?

A. 2

B. 5

C. 9

D. 12

9) If $\frac{3x}{2} = 15$, then $\frac{2x}{5} = ?$

A. 4

B. 8

C. 10

D. 20

10) The price of a car was $20,000 in 2014, and it was $15,000 in 2015. What is the rate of depreciation of the price of car per year?

A. 15%

B. 25%

C. 30%

D. 35%

11) Which of the following is the greatest number?

A. $\frac{1}{4}$

B. $\frac{7}{9}$

C. 0.85

D. 75%

12) Calculate the approximate area of the following circle. (The diameter of the circle is 10 cm)

A. 1250 cm^2

B. 314cm^2

C. 116 cm^2

D. 78.5 cm^2

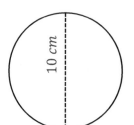

13) 90 is equal to?

A. $2 + (3 \times 10) + (2 \times 30)$

B. $\left(\frac{10}{3} \times 27\right) + (\frac{5}{2} \times 2)$

C. $((\frac{3}{2} + 3) \times \frac{18}{3}) + 63$

D. $(2 \times 15) + (50 \times 2) - 46$

14) Which of the following angles can represent the three angles of an isosceles right triangle?

A. $45°, 90°, 45°$

B. $50°, 50°, 80°$

C. $60°, 60°, 60°$

D. $55°, 35°, 90°$

15) If 120% of a number is 84, then what is 90% of that number?

A. 45

B. 63

C. 74

D. 84

16) What is the missing term in the given numbers?

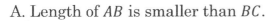

$$3, 4, 6, 9, 13, 18, 24, \underline{\quad}, 39$$

A. 24

B. 26

C. 27

D. 31

17) In following rectangle which statement is true?

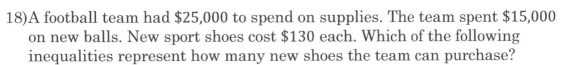

A. Length of AB is smaller than BC.

B. The sum of all the angles equals 360 degrees.

C. Length of AB equal to length DC.

D. AB is perpendicular to DC.

18) A football team had $25,000 to spend on supplies. The team spent $15,000 on new balls. New sport shoes cost $130 each. Which of the following inequalities represent how many new shoes the team can purchase?

A. $130x + 15,000 \leq 25,000$

B. $130x + 15,000 \geq 25,000$

C. $15,000x + 130 \leq 25,000$

D. $15,000x + 130 \geq 25,000$

19) The capacity of a red box is 30% greater than a blue box. If the capacity of the red box is 52 books, how many books can be put in the blue box?

A. 9

B. 15

C. 40

D. 42

20) From last year, the price of gasoline has increased from $1.40 per gallon to $1.75 per gallon. The new price is what percent of the original price?

A. 72%

B. 125%

C. 140%

D. 160%

21) When a gas tank can hold 30 gallons, how many gallons does it contain when it is $\frac{2}{3}$ full?

A. 115

B. 65.5

C. 20

D. 10

22) 190 minutes = …?

A. 3.25 *Hours*

B. 3.16 *Hours*

C. 2 *Hours*

D. 0.4 *Hours*

23) Which of the following is **NOT** a prime number?

A. 107

B. 101

C. 71

D. 58

24) What is the perimeter of a square that has an area of 36 square inches?

A. 144 inches

B. 36 inches

C. 24 inches

D. 56 inches

25) Jason left a $13.00 tip on a lunch that cost $26.00, what percentage was the tip?

A. 2.5%

B. 10%

C. 25%

D. 50%

26) A box of 36 pencils costs $1.80, what is the unit cost?

A. $0.50

B. $0.25

C. $0.08

D. $0.05

27) Two-kilograms apple and two-kilograms orange cost $26.4 If one-kilogram apple costs $4.2 how much does one-kilogram orange cost?

A. $9

B. $6

C. $4.5

D. $4

28) $[6 \times (-24) + 8] - (-4) + [6 \times 5] \div 2 = ?$

A. 158

B. 132

C. -104

D. -117

29) The width of a rectangle is $3x$ and its length is $5x$. The perimeter of the rectangle is 80. What is the value of x?

A. 4

B. 5

C. 6

D. 10

30) Jason is 15 miles ahead of Joe running at 5.5 miles per hour and Joe is running at the speed of 7 miles per hour. How long does it take Joe to catch Jason?

A. 4 hours

B. 6 *hours*

C. 8*hours*

D. 10 *hours*

31) $\Big(\big((-12) + 20\big) \times 3\Big) + (-16)$?

A. 1

B. 4

C. 6

D. 8

32) If 45% of a class are girls, and 20% of girls play tennis, what percent of the class play tennis?

A. 9%

B. 15%

C. 25%

D. 40%

33) The price of a sofa is decreased by 30% to $490. What was its original price?

A. $480

B. $510

C. $550

D. $700

34) In a class, there are twice as many boys as girls. If the total number of students in the class is 45, how many girls are in the class?

A. 15

B. 25

C. 30

D. 35

35) At a Zoo, the ratio of lions to tigers is 5 to 3. Which of the following could NOT be the total number of lions and tigers in the zoo?

A. 32

B. 40

C. 97

D. 104

36) Solving the equation: $10x - 15.5 = -55.5$?

A. -4

B. -3

C. 4

D. 3

37) A shaft rotates 400 times in 5 seconds. How many times does it rotate in 0.25 minutes?

A. 1,200

B. 950

C. 400

D. 100

38) A swimming pool holds 2,500 cubic feet of water. The swimming pool is 40 feet long and 10 feet wide. How deep is the swimming pool?

A. 6.25 feet

B. 12 feet

C. 40 feet

D. 100 feet

39) What is the value of x in the following equation?

$$6^x = 7,776$$

A. 3

B. 4

C. 5

D. 6

40) What is the value of x in the following equation?

$$10 + 5(x + 5 - 5x) = 40$$

A. -3

B. $-\frac{1}{4}$

C. $\frac{1}{4}$

D. 3

41) What is the area of the trapezoid?

A. 25

B. 45

C. 100

D. 150

42) 13.125 ÷ 0.005?

A. 2.625

B. 26.25

C. 262.5

D. 2,625

43) A card is drawn at random from a standard 52–card deck, what is the probability that the card is of Hearts? (The deck includes 13 of each suit clubs, diamonds, hearts, and spades)

A. $\frac{1}{3}$

B. $\frac{1}{4}$

C. $\frac{1}{6}$

D. $\frac{1}{78}$

44) Ella bought a pair of gloves for $13.59. She gave the clerk $20.00. How much change should she get back?

A. $4.51

B. $6.41

C. $7.51

D. $8.51

45) $\frac{5 \times 20}{80}$ is closest estimate to?

A. 1.01

B. 1.1

C. 1.3

D. 1.4

46) If 60% of A is 30% of B, then B is what percent of A?

A. 2%

B. 20%

C. 200%

D. 300%

47) $\dfrac{3}{4} + \dfrac{\frac{-3}{5}}{\frac{6}{10}} = ?$

A. $\dfrac{1}{4}$

B. $\dfrac{1}{2}$

C. $-\dfrac{1}{4}$

D. $-\dfrac{1}{2}$

IF YOU FINISH BEFORE TIME IS CALLED, YOU MAY CHECK YOUR WORK ON THIS SECTION.

STOP

ISEE Middle Level Math Practice Test 2

2022 - 2023

Two Parts

Total number of questions: 84

Part 1 (Quantitative Reasoning): 37 questions

Part 2 (Mathematics Achievement): 47 questions

Total time for two parts: 75 Minutes

120

ISEE Middle Level Practice Test Answer Sheets

Remove (or photocopy) this answer sheet and use it to complete the practice test.

ISEE Middle Level Practice Test 2

Quantitative Reasoning

1	Ⓐ Ⓑ Ⓒ Ⓓ	25	Ⓐ Ⓑ Ⓒ Ⓓ
2	Ⓐ Ⓑ Ⓒ Ⓓ	26	Ⓐ Ⓑ Ⓒ Ⓓ
3	Ⓐ Ⓑ Ⓒ Ⓓ	27	Ⓐ Ⓑ Ⓒ Ⓓ
4	Ⓐ Ⓑ Ⓒ Ⓓ	28	Ⓐ Ⓑ Ⓒ Ⓓ
5	Ⓐ Ⓑ Ⓒ Ⓓ	29	Ⓐ Ⓑ Ⓒ Ⓓ
6	Ⓐ Ⓑ Ⓒ Ⓓ	30	Ⓐ Ⓑ Ⓒ Ⓓ
7	Ⓐ Ⓑ Ⓒ Ⓓ	31	Ⓐ Ⓑ Ⓒ Ⓓ
8	Ⓐ Ⓑ Ⓒ Ⓓ	32	Ⓐ Ⓑ Ⓒ Ⓓ
9	Ⓐ Ⓑ Ⓒ Ⓓ	33	Ⓐ Ⓑ Ⓒ Ⓓ
10	Ⓐ Ⓑ Ⓒ Ⓓ	34	Ⓐ Ⓑ Ⓒ Ⓓ
11	Ⓐ Ⓑ Ⓒ Ⓓ	35	Ⓐ Ⓑ Ⓒ Ⓓ
12	Ⓐ Ⓑ Ⓒ Ⓓ	36	Ⓐ Ⓑ Ⓒ Ⓓ
13	Ⓐ Ⓑ Ⓒ Ⓓ	37	Ⓐ Ⓑ Ⓒ Ⓓ
14	Ⓐ Ⓑ Ⓒ Ⓓ		
15	Ⓐ Ⓑ Ⓒ Ⓓ		
16	Ⓐ Ⓑ Ⓒ Ⓓ		
17	Ⓐ Ⓑ Ⓒ Ⓓ		
18	Ⓐ Ⓑ Ⓒ Ⓓ		
19	Ⓐ Ⓑ Ⓒ Ⓓ		
20	Ⓐ Ⓑ Ⓒ Ⓓ		
21	Ⓐ Ⓑ Ⓒ Ⓓ		
22	Ⓐ Ⓑ Ⓒ Ⓓ		
23	Ⓐ Ⓑ Ⓒ Ⓓ		
24	Ⓐ Ⓑ Ⓒ Ⓓ		

Mathematics Achievement

1	Ⓐ Ⓑ Ⓒ Ⓓ	25	Ⓐ Ⓑ Ⓒ Ⓓ
2	Ⓐ Ⓑ Ⓒ Ⓓ	26	Ⓐ Ⓑ Ⓒ Ⓓ
3	Ⓐ Ⓑ Ⓒ Ⓓ	27	Ⓐ Ⓑ Ⓒ Ⓓ
4	Ⓐ Ⓑ Ⓒ Ⓓ	28	Ⓐ Ⓑ Ⓒ Ⓓ
5	Ⓐ Ⓑ Ⓒ Ⓓ	29	Ⓐ Ⓑ Ⓒ Ⓓ
6	Ⓐ Ⓑ Ⓒ Ⓓ	30	Ⓐ Ⓑ Ⓒ Ⓓ
7	Ⓐ Ⓑ Ⓒ Ⓓ	31	Ⓐ Ⓑ Ⓒ Ⓓ
8	Ⓐ Ⓑ Ⓒ Ⓓ	32	Ⓐ Ⓑ Ⓒ Ⓓ
9	Ⓐ Ⓑ Ⓒ Ⓓ	33	Ⓐ Ⓑ Ⓒ Ⓓ
10	Ⓐ Ⓑ Ⓒ Ⓓ	34	Ⓐ Ⓑ Ⓒ Ⓓ
11	Ⓐ Ⓑ Ⓒ Ⓓ	35	Ⓐ Ⓑ Ⓒ Ⓓ
12	Ⓐ Ⓑ Ⓒ Ⓓ	36	Ⓐ Ⓑ Ⓒ Ⓓ
13	Ⓐ Ⓑ Ⓒ Ⓓ	37	Ⓐ Ⓑ Ⓒ Ⓓ
14	Ⓐ Ⓑ Ⓒ Ⓓ	38	Ⓐ Ⓑ Ⓒ Ⓓ
15	Ⓐ Ⓑ Ⓒ Ⓓ	39	Ⓐ Ⓑ Ⓒ Ⓓ
16	Ⓐ Ⓑ Ⓒ Ⓓ	40	Ⓐ Ⓑ Ⓒ Ⓓ
17	Ⓐ Ⓑ Ⓒ Ⓓ	41	Ⓐ Ⓑ Ⓒ Ⓓ
18	Ⓐ Ⓑ Ⓒ Ⓓ	42	Ⓐ Ⓑ Ⓒ Ⓓ
19	Ⓐ Ⓑ Ⓒ Ⓓ	43	Ⓐ Ⓑ Ⓒ Ⓓ
20	Ⓐ Ⓑ Ⓒ Ⓓ	44	Ⓐ Ⓑ Ⓒ Ⓓ
21	Ⓐ Ⓑ Ⓒ Ⓓ	45	Ⓐ Ⓑ Ⓒ Ⓓ
22	Ⓐ Ⓑ Ⓒ Ⓓ	46	Ⓐ Ⓑ Ⓒ Ⓓ
23	Ⓐ Ⓑ Ⓒ Ⓓ	47	Ⓐ Ⓑ Ⓒ Ⓓ
24	Ⓐ Ⓑ Ⓒ Ⓓ		

ISEE Middle Level Math
Practice Test 2

Section 1

37 questions

Total time for this section: 35 Minutes

You may NOT use a calculator for this test

1) What is the value of x in the following equation?

$$\frac{7^x}{7} = 343$$

A. 4

B. 5

C. 8

D. 12

2) In following shape y equals to?

A. 120°

B. 30°

C. 25.5°

D. 20°

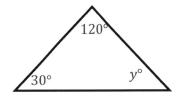

3) Which of the following shows the numbers in increasing order?

A. $\frac{1}{3}, \frac{8}{12}, \frac{4}{7}, \frac{3}{4}$

B. $\frac{1}{3}, \frac{4}{7}, \frac{8}{12}, \frac{3}{4}$

C. $\frac{4}{7}, \frac{3}{4}, \frac{8}{12}, \frac{1}{3}$

D. $\frac{8}{12}, \frac{3}{4}, \frac{4}{7}, \frac{1}{3}$

4) If an object travels at 0.4 cm per second, how many meters does it travel in 5 hours?

A. 88.2 m

B. 76.4 m

C. 72 m

D. 43.2 m

5) If the ratio of home fans to visiting fans in a crowd is 3 : 2 and all 24,000 seats in a stadium are filled, how many visiting fans are in attendance?

A. 96,000

B. 9,600

C. 960

D. 96

6) What's the approximate circumference of a circle that has a diameter of 17 m?

A. 53.38 m

B. 71.9 m

C. 97.25 m

D. 100 m

7) What is the lowest common multiple of 24 and 36?

A. 48

B. 72

C. 108

D. 864

8) What is the area of the shaded region? (one fourth of the circle is shaded) (Diameter = 8)

A. 4 π

B. 6 π

C. 8 π

D. 9 π

9) An item in the store originally priced at $200 was marked down 30%. What is the final sale price of the item?

A. $240

B. $204

C. $200

D. $140

10) A shirt costing $300 is discounted 15%. After a month, the shirt is discounted another 25%. Which of the following expressions can be used to find the selling price of the shirt?

A. (300) (0.70)

B. (300) − 300 (0.30)

C. (300)(0.15) − (400) (0.15)

D. (300) (0.85) (0.75)

11) If a car has 70-liter petrol and after one hour driving the car use 5-liter petrol, how much petrol remaining after x-hours?

A. $5x - 70$

B. $70 + 5x$

C. $70 - 5x$

D. $70 - x$

12) Solve for x: $4 + x + 8\left(\frac{x}{4}\right) = 2x + 12$

A. 8

B. 5.5

C. 4

D. 4.5

13) The area of the trapezoid below is 136. What is the value of x?

A. 7

B. 8

C. 10

D. 11

14) Find $\frac{1}{3}$ of $\frac{1}{2}$ of $\frac{3}{5}$ of 280?

A. 28

B. 30

C. 31

D. 2

15) If $x \leq a$ is the solution of $6 + 3x \leq 21$, what is the value of a?

A. $21x$

B. 5

C. -5

D. $15x$

16) 7 liters of water are poured into an aquarium that's $25cm$ long, $5cm$ wide, and $70cm$ high. How many cm will the water level in the aquarium rise due to this added water? ($1\ liter\ of\ water\ =\ 1,000\ cm^3$)

A. 80

B. 56

C. 49

D. 10

17) If $4f + 4g = 4x - 2y$ and $g = 2y - 6x$, what is $2f$?

A. $5x + y$

B. $14x + 3y$

C. $14x - 5y$

D. $y - 3x$

18) What is the value of $\dfrac{-\frac{13}{3} \times \frac{4}{5}}{\frac{10}{30}}$?

A. -10.4

B. 10.4

C. $-\dfrac{1}{9}$

D. $\dfrac{1}{9}$

19) What is the perimeter of the following parallelogram?

A. 54

B. 44

C. 24

D. 17

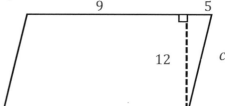

20) In a bundle of 50 fruits, 6 are apples and the rest are bananas. What percent of the bundle is composed of apples?

A. 30%

B. 25%

C. 12%

D. 10%

21) 3 less than twice a positive integer is 71. What is the integer?

A. 37

B. 40

C. 42

D. 44

22) If Joe was making $8.50 per hour and got a raise of $0.35 per hour, approximately what percentage increase was the raise?

A. 2%

B. 2.67%

C. 3.33%

D. 4.00%

23) Which is the equivalent temperature of $140°F$ in Celsius? ($C = Celsius$)

$$C = \frac{5}{9}(F - 32)$$

A. 32

B. 38.5

C. 50

D. 60

24) The average of $14, 16, 21$ and x is 20. What is the value of x?

A. 9

B. 15

C. 18

D. 29

25) What is the value of mode and median in the following set of numbers?

$$2, 3, 3, 6, 5, 5, 4, 4, 6, 2, 2$$

A. Mode: 2 Median:4

B. Mode:2, Median:4

C. Mode:2, 3 Median:5

D. Mode: 3 Median:4

Quantitative Comparisons

Direction: Questions 26 to 37 are Quantitative Comparisons Questions. Using the information provided in each question, compare the quantity in column A to the quantity in Column B. Choose on your answer sheet grid

A   if the quantity in Column A is greater

B   if the quantity in Column B is greater

C   if the two quantities are equal

D   if the relationship cannot be determined from the information given

26)

Column A	Column B
$\dfrac{\sqrt{64-48}}{\sqrt{25-9}}$	$\dfrac{(7-4)}{(8-3)}$

27) $2x^5 - 9 = 477$

$$\frac{1}{3} - \frac{y}{5} = -\frac{7}{15}$$

Column A	Column B
x	y

28) The sum of 3 consecutive integers is -45.

Column A	Column B
The largest of these integers	-16

29)

Column A	Column B
$4^2 - 2^4$	$2^4 - 4^2$

30) A computer costs $250.

Column A	Column B
A sales tax at 8% of the computer cost	$20

31)

Column A	Column B
The slope of the line $4x + 2y = 7$	The slope of the line that passes through points $(2, 5)$ and $(3, 3)$

32)

Column A	Column B
The least prime factor of 55	The least prime factor of 210

33)

Column A	Column B
$\sqrt{144 - 81}$	$\sqrt{144} - \sqrt{81}$

34) 6 percent of x is equal to 5 percent of y, where x and y are positive numbers.

Column A	Column B
x	y

35)

Column A	Column B
$(-5)^4$	5^4

36)

Column A	Column B
$(1.88)^4(1.88)^8$	$(1.88)^{12}$

37) x is a positive number.

Column A	Column B
x^{10}	x^{20}

IF YOU FINISH BEFORE TIME IS CALLED, YOU MAY CHECK YOUR WORK ON THIS SECTION ONLY. DO NOT TURN TO OTHER SECTION IN THE TEST.   STOP

ISEE Middle Level Math
Practice Test 2

Section 2

47 questions

Total time for this section: 40 Minutes

You may NOT use a calculator for this test.

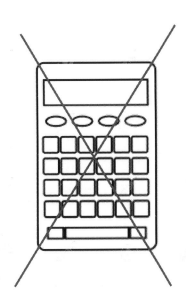

1) Which of the following is not synonym for 20^2?

A. 20 cubed

B. 20 squared

C. The square of 20

D. 20 to the second power

2) What is the value of x in the following equation?

$$3^x + 28 = 55$$

A. 3

B. 4

C. 5

D. 6

3) If angles A and B are angles of a parallelogram, what is the sum of the measures of the two angles?

A. 360 degrees

B. 180 degrees

C. 90 degrees

D. Cannot be determined

4) If $x =$ lowest common multiple of 10 and 35, then $\frac{x}{5} + 2$ equal to?

A. 70

B. 58

C. 46

D. 16

5) If the area of the following trapezoid is 30, what is the perimeter of the trapezoid?

A. 25

B. 28

C. 45

D. 55

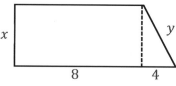

6) A swing moves from one extreme point (point *A*) to the opposite extreme point (point *B*) in 20 seconds. How long does it take that the swing moves 5 times from point *A* to point *B* and returns to point *A*?

A. 400 seconds

B. 200 seconds

C. 150 seconds

D. 100 seconds

7) There are 2 cars moving in the same direction on a road. A red car is 12 *km* ahead of a blue car. If the speed of the red car is 40 *km per hour* and the speed of the blue car is $1\frac{2}{5}$ of the red car, how many minutes will it take the blue car to catch the red car?

A. 8.5

B. 15

C. 30

D. 45

8) In two successive years, the population of a town is increased by 10% and 25%. What percent of the population is increased after two years?

A. 25%

B. 35%

C. 36%

D. 37%

9) $5 + 8 \times (-2) - [4 + 22 \times 5] \div 6 = ?$

A. 120

B. 88

C. −30

D. −20

10) In 1989, the average worker's income increased $2,500 per year starting from $26,000 annual salary. Which equation represents income greater than average?

(I = income, x = number of years after 1989)

A. $I > 2,500x + 26,000$

B. $I > -2,500x + 26,000$

C. $I < -2,500x + 26,000$

D. $I < 2,500x - 26,000$

11) Which of the following angles is obtuse?

A. 10 degrees

B. 30 degrees

C. 189 degrees

D. 120 degrees

12) Mr. Jones saves $2,500 out of his monthly family income of $65,000. What fractional part of his income does he save?

A. $\dfrac{1}{26}$

B. $\dfrac{1}{11}$

C. $\dfrac{3}{26}$

D. $\dfrac{2}{15}$

13) Anita's trick–or–treat bag contains 13 pieces of chocolate, 19 suckers, 19 pieces of gum, 25 pieces of licorice. If she randomly pulls a piece of candy from her bag, what is the probability of her pulling out a piece of sucker

A. $\dfrac{1}{3}$

B. $\dfrac{1}{4}$

C. $\dfrac{1}{5}$

D. $\dfrac{1}{19}$

14) 110 is equal to?

A. $20 - (4 \times 10) + (6 \times 30)$

B. $\left(\frac{11}{8} \times 72\right) + \left(\frac{125}{5}\right)$

C. $\left(\left(\frac{30}{4} + \frac{13}{2}\right) \times 7\right) - \frac{11}{2} + \frac{110}{4}$

D. $(2 \times 10) + (50 \times 1.5) + 15$

15) What is the difference in area between a 8 cm by 4 cm rectangle and a circle with diameter of 8 cm? ($\pi = 3$)

A. 49 cm

B. 40 cm

C. 39 cm

D. 16 cm

16) Solve the following equation?

$$(x^2 + 2x + 1) = 64$$

A. $-9, -7$

B. $-9, 7$

C. -9

D. 7

17) What is ratio of perimeter of figure A to area of figure B?

A. $\frac{1}{3}$

B. $\frac{3}{8}$

C. 3

D. 5

Fig. A Fig. B

18) $\frac{18 \times 21}{5}$ is closest estimate to?

A. 75.6

B. 68.7

C. 50.6

D. 40.7

19) How many possible outfit combinations come from four shirts, two slacks, and five ties?

A. 60

B. 40

C. 16

D. 10

20) When a number is multiplied to itself and added by 9, the result is 25. What is the value of the number?

A. 4 or −4

B. 5 or −5

C. 4

D. 5

21) If you invest $2,000 at an annual rate of 8%, how much interest will you earn after one year?

A. 16,000

B. 16,00

C. 380

D. 160

22) What is the value of x in the equation: $\frac{x}{4} + \frac{5}{4} = 5$?

A. 15

B. 10

C. 8

D. 5

23) If $y = 5ab + 3b^3$, what is y when $a = 3$ and $b = 2$?

A. 64

B. 65

C. 55

D. 54

24) What is the absolute value of the quantity six minus ten?

A. −4

B. 10

C. −10

D. 4

25) Which of the following angles can represent the three angles of an equilateral triangle?

A. $45°, 90°, 45°$

B. $50°, 50°, 80°$

C. $60°, 60°, 60°$

D. $55°, 35°, 90°$

26) In the following equation, what is the value of $x + y$?

$$9x - 10 = 5\left(\frac{4}{5}x - y\right) + 5$$

A. 15

B. −15

C. 3

D. −3

27) How many tiles of $3\ cm^2$ is needed to cover a floor of dimension $7\ cm$ by $27\ cm$?

A. 12

B. 38

C. 63

D. 66

28) Two-kilogram apple and three-kilograms orange cost $21. If the price of one-kilogram of apple is twice the price of one-kilogram of orange, how much does one-kilogram apple cost?

A. $8

B. $6

C. $4

D. $1

29) Which is **NOT** a prime number?

A. 181

B. 151

C. 131

D. 122

30) Each of the x students in a team may invite up to 6 friends to a party. What is the maximum number of students and guests who might attend the party?

A. $6x + 6$

B. $6x$

C. $x + 6$

D. $7x$

31) Calculate the approximate circumference of the following circle. (the diameter is 10)

A. 1,267

B. 314

C. 31

D. 10

32) 280 *minutes* = ...?

A. 5 *Hours*

B. 4.6 *Hours*

C. 3.5 *Hours*

D. 0.5 *Hours*

33) There are three boxes, a red box, a blue box, and a yellow box. If the weight of the red box is 60 kg and it is 80% of the weight of the blue box, and the weight of the blue box is 120% of the weight of the yellow box, what is the weight of all boxes?

A. 197.5 kg

B. 210.5 kg

C. 280 kg

D. 320 kg

34) In the figure below, line *A* is parallel to line *B*. What is the value of angle *x*?

A. 35 degree

B. 40 degree

C. 100 degree

D. 140 degree

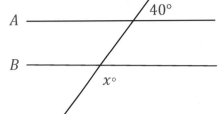

35) Jim drove 350 miles and it took him approximately 9 hours. How many miles per hour was his average speed?

A. about 34.7 miles per hour

B. about 38.8 miles per hour

C. about 48.5 miles per hour

D. about 49.5 miles per hour

36) Three people go to a restaurant. Their bill comes to $58.00. They decided to split the cost. One person pays $7.5, the next person pays 2 times that amount. How much will the third person have to pay?

A. $34.50

B. $35.50

C. $41.00

D. $45.00

37) $\left(\left((-15) + 40\right) \times \frac{1}{5}\right) + (-15)?$

A. 5

B. 10

C. −5

D. −10

38) What is 13,8210 in scientific notation?

A. 138.21×10^3

B. 13.821×10^4

C. 0.13821×10^6

D. 1.3821×10^5

39) What is the value of $(10 - 6)!$?

A. 20

B. 24

C. 26

D. 28

40) What is the perimeter of the below right triangle?

A. 20

B. 18

C. 15

D. 12

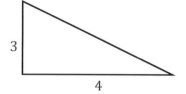

41) If 150% of a number is equal to 30% of 80, then what is the number?

A. 16

B. 15.5

C. 14.66

D. 12.25

42) In a department of a company, the ratio of employees with Bachelor's Degree to employees with high school Diploma is 1 to 4. If there are 24 employees with Bachelor's Degree in this department, how many employees with High School Diploma should be moved to other departments to change the ratio of the number of employees with Bachelor's Degree to the number of employees with High School Diploma to 3 to 4 in this department?

A. 64

B. 54

C. 10

D. 12

43) What is x in the following right triangle?

A. $\sqrt{399}$

B. 15

C. 20

D. $\sqrt{402}$

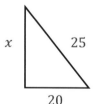

44) The average weight of 20 girls in a class is 65 kg and the average weight of 35 boys in the same class is 72 kg. What is the average weight of all the 55 students in that class?

A. 61.28

B. 61.68

C. 62.90

D. 69.45

45) An angle is equal to one ninth of its supplement. What is the measure of that angle?

A. 18

B. 30

C. 45

D. 60

46) What is the difference of smallest 5–digit number and biggest 5–digit number?

A. 66,666

B. 67,899

C. 88,888

D. 89,999

47) John traveled 140 km in 5 hours and Alice traveled 210 km in 3 hours. What is the ratio of the average speed of John to average speed of Alice?

A. 2 : 5

B. 5 : 2

C. 5 : 9

D. 5 : 6

IF YOU FINISH BEFORE TIME IS CALLED, YOU MAY CHECK YOUR WORK ON THIS SECTION.   STOP

ISEE Middle Level Practice Tests Answer Keys

Now, it's time to review your results to see where you went wrong and what areas you need to improve!

ISEE Middle Level Math Practice Test 1 Answer Key									
Quantitative Reasoning						**Mathematics Achievement**			
1	B	17	C	33	D	1	C	17	B	33	D
2	B	18	C	34	D	2	C	18	A	34	A
3	B	19	C	35	C	3	A	19	C	35	C
4	A	20	D	36	A	4	D	20	B	36	A
5	D	21	D	37	D	5	D	21	C	37	A
6	C	22	A			6	B	22	B	38	A
7	B	23	A			7	C	23	D	39	C
8	D	24	A			8	C	24	C	40	B
9	A	25	A			9	A	25	D	41	B
10	B	26	A			10	B	26	D	42	D
11	D	27	B			11	C	27	A	43	B
12	D	28	A			12	D	28	D	44	B
13	D	29	D			13	C	29	B	45	C
14	D	30	A			14	A	30	D	46	C
15	D	31	A			15	B	31	D	47	C
16	B	32	A			16	D	32	A		

ISEE Middle Level Math Practice Test 2 Answer Key

Quantitative Reasoning						Mathematics Achievement					
1	A	17	C	33	A	1	A	17	C	33	A
2	B	18	A	34	B	2	A	18	A	34	D
3	B	19	A	35	C	3	D	19	B	35	B
4	C	20	C	36	C	4	D	20	A	36	B
5	B	21	A	37	D	5	B	21	D	37	D
6	A	22	D			6	B	22	A	38	D
7	B	23	D			7	D	23	D	39	B
8	A	24	D			8	D	24	D	40	D
9	D	25	B			9	C	25	C	41	A
10	D	26	A			10	A	26	C	42	A
11	C	27	B			11	D	27	C	43	B
12	A	28	A			12	A	28	B	44	D
13	B	29	C			13	B	29	D	45	A
14	A	30	C			14	D	30	D	46	D
15	B	31	C			15	D	31	C	47	A
16	B	32	A			16	B	32	B		

Score Your Test

ISEE scores are broken down by its four sections: Verbal Reasoning, Reading Comprehension, Quantitative Reasoning, and Mathematics Achievement. A sum of the three sections is also reported.

For the Middle Level ISEE, the score range is 760 to 940, the lowest possible score a student can earn is 760 and the highest score is 940 for each section. A student receives 1 point for every correct answer. There is no penalty for wrong or skipped questions.

The total scaled score for a Middle Level ISEE test is the sum of the scores for all sections. A student will also receive a percentile score of between 1-99% that compares that student's test scores with those of other test takers of same grade and gender from the past 3 years.

Use the next table to convert ISEE Middle level raw score to scaled score for application to 7th and 8th grade.

ISEE Middle Level Scaled Scores

Raw Score	Quantitative Reasoning		Mathematics Achievement		Raw Score	Quantitative Reasoning		Mathematics Achievement	
	7th Grade	8th Grade	7th Grade	8th Grade		7th Grade	8th Grade	7th Grade	8th Grade
0	760	760	760	760	26	900	885	885	865
1	770	765	770	765	27	905	890	885	865
2	780	770	780	770	28	910	895	890	870
3	790	775	790	775	29	910	900	890	870
4	800	780	800	780	30	915	905	895	875
5	810	785	810	785	31	920	910	895	875
6	820	790	820	790	32	925	915	900	880
7	825	795	825	795	33	930	920	900	880
8	830	800	830	800	34	930	925	905	885
9	835	805	835	805	35	935	930	905	885
10	840	810	840	810	36	935	935	910	890
11	845	815	845	815	37	940	940	910	890
12	850	820	850	820	38			915	895
13	855	825	855	825	39			920	900
14	860	830	855	830	40			925	905
15	865	835	860	835	41			925	910
16	870	840	860	840	42			930	915
17	875	845	865	840	43			930	920
18	880	845	865	845	44			935	925
19	880	850	870	845	45			935	930
20	885	855	870	850	46			940	935
21	885	860	875	850	47			940	940
22	890	865	875	855					
23	890	870	875	855					
24	895	875	880	860					
25	895	880	880	860					

ISEE Middle Level Practice Tests Answers and Explanations

ISEE Middle LEVEL Math Practice Test 1 Section 1

1) Choice B is correct

$$\frac{-50 \times 0.5}{5} = -\frac{50 \times \frac{1}{2}}{5} = -\frac{\frac{50}{2}}{5} = -\frac{50}{10} = -5$$

2) Choice B is correct

Use the formula for Percent of Change: $\frac{New\ Value - Old\ Value}{Old\ Value} \times 100\%$

$\frac{29-41}{41} \times 100 = -29\%$ (negative sign here means that the new price is less than old price)

3) Choice B is correct

$$562,357,741 \times \frac{1}{10,000} = 56235.7741$$

4) Choice A is correct

30% off equals $24. Let x be the original price of the table. Then:

$$30\%\ of\ x = 24 \rightarrow 0.3x = 24 \rightarrow x = \frac{24}{0.3} = 80$$

5) Choice D is correct

$3f = 3 \times (3x - 2y) = 9x - 6y, 3f + g = 9x - 6y + x + 5y = 10x - y$

6) Choice C is correct

$\frac{1}{7} \approx 0.14; \frac{1}{3} \approx 0.33; \frac{3}{5} = 0.6; \frac{3}{4} = 0.75$

7) Choice B is correct

$8^x = 512$, and $512 = 8^3 \rightarrow x = 3$

8) Choice D is correct

Supplementary angles sum up to 180 degrees. x and 35 degrees are supplementary angles. Then: $x = 180° - 35° = 145°$

9) Choice A is correct

If the score of Mia was 40, therefore the score of Ava is 20. Since, the score of Emma was half as that of Ava, therefore, the score of Emma is 10.

10) Choice B is correct

Use the formula of areas of circles. *Area of a circle* $= \pi r^2 \Rightarrow 49\pi = \pi r^2 \Rightarrow 49 = r^2 \Rightarrow r = 7$, Radius of the circle is 7 Now, use the circumference formula:

Circumference $= 2\pi r = 2\pi\,(7) = 14\,\pi$

11) Choice D is correct

Let x be the number. Write the equation and solve for x. $\frac{2}{3} \times 15 = \frac{5}{2} \times x \Rightarrow \frac{2 \times 15}{3} = \frac{5x}{2}$, use cross multiplication to solve for x. $2 \times 30 = 5x \times 3 \Rightarrow 60 = 15x \Rightarrow x = 4$

12) Choice D is correct

$1.15 = \frac{115}{100}$ and $\quad 8.2 = \frac{82}{10} \rightarrow 1.15 \times 8.2 = \frac{115}{100} \times \frac{82}{10} = \frac{9,430}{1,000} = 9.43 \approx 9.4$

13) Choice D is correct

The perimeter of the trapezoid is 56.

Therefore, the missing side is $= 56 - 17 - 16 - 8 = 15$

Area of a trapezoid: $A = \frac{1}{2}h(b_1 + b_2) = \frac{1}{2}(15)(8 + 16) = \frac{1}{2}(15)(24) = 180$

14) Choice D is correct

Add the first 5 numbers. $42 + 46 + 52 + 35 + 58 = 233$

To find the distance traveled in the next 5 hours, multiply the average by number of hours.

Distance = Average $\times$ Rate $= 60 \times 5 = 300$, Add both numbers. $300 + 233 = 533$

15) Choice D is correct

$average = \frac{10+13+29+37+46+66+100+124}{8} = 53.12$

16) Choice B is correct

$\frac{2}{5}$ of $145 = \frac{2}{5} \times 145 = 58, \frac{1}{2}$ of $58 = \frac{1}{2} \times 58 = 29$

17) Choice C is correct

Let x be the original price. If the price of a laptop is decreased by 20% to \$320, then: 80% of $x = 320 \Rightarrow 0.80x = 320 \Rightarrow x = 320 \div 0.80 = 400$

18) Choice C is correct

Let x be the sales profit. Then, 3% of sales profit is $0.03x$. Employee's revenue: $0.03x + 7,500$

19) Choice C is correct

The ratio of boy to girls is $7: 4$. Therefore, there are 7 boys out of 11 students. To find the answer, first divide the total number of students by 11, then multiply the result by 7.

$44 \div 11 = 4 \Rightarrow 4 \times 7 = 28$, There are 28 boys and 16 $(44 - 28)$ girls. So, 12 more girls should be enrolled to make the ratio $1:1$

20) Choice D is correct

Let's review the choices:

A. $\frac{3}{5} > 0.8$ This is not a correct statement. Because $\frac{3}{5} = 0.6$ and it's less than 0.8.

B. $12\% = \frac{2}{5}$ This is not a correct statement. Because $12\% = 0.12$ and $\frac{2}{5} = 0.4$

C. $3 < \frac{5}{2}$ This is not a correct statement. Because $\frac{5}{2} = 2.5$ and it's less than 3.

D. $\frac{7}{6} > 0.8$ This is a correct statement. $\frac{7}{6} = 1.16 \rightarrow 0.8 < \frac{7}{6}$

21) Choice D is correct

Simplify: $6(x + 1) = 4(x - 4) + 20$, $6x + 6 = 4x - 16 + 20$, $6x + 6 = 4x + 4$

Subtract $4x$ from both sides: $2x + 6 = 4$, Add 4 to both sides: $-2 = 2x$, $-1 = x$

22) Choice A is correct

$x = 25 + 135 = 160$

23) Choice A is correct

Petrol of car A in $350\ km = \frac{4 \times 350}{140} = 10$, Petrol of car B in $350km = \frac{3 \times 350}{140} = 7.5$, $10 - 7.5 = 2.5$

24) Choice A is correct

The diagonal of the square is 6. Let x be the side.

Use Pythagorean Theorem: $a^2 + b^2 = c^2$

$x^2 + x^2 = 6^2 \Rightarrow 2x^2 = 6^2 \Rightarrow 2x^2 = 36 \Rightarrow x^2 = 18 \Rightarrow x = \sqrt{18}$

The area of the square is: $\sqrt{18} \times \sqrt{18} = 18$

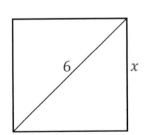

25) Choice A is correct

$-25 - (-66) = -25 + 66 = 66 - 25 = 41$

26) Choice A is correct.

Column A: Simplify. $\sqrt{36} + \sqrt{36} = 6 + 6 = 12$, 12 is greater than $\sqrt{72}$ ($\sqrt{144} = 12$)

27) Choice B is correct.

Column A: The value of x when $y = 12$:

$y = -4x - 8 \rightarrow 12 = -4x - 8 \rightarrow -4x = 20 \rightarrow x = -5$

Column B: -4, -4 is greater than -5.

28) Choice A is correct.

Column A: Use order of operation to calculate the result.

$6 + 4 \times 7 + 8 = 6 + 28 + 8 = 42$

Column B: $4 + 6 \times 7 - 8 \rightarrow 4 + 42 - 8 = 38$

29) Choice D is correct.

Column A: Based on information provided, we cannot find the average age of Joe and Michelle or average age of Michelle and Nicole.

30) Choice A is correct.

Column A: Simplify. $\sqrt{121 - 64} = \sqrt{57}$

Column B: $\sqrt{121} - \sqrt{64} = 11 - 8 = 3$, $\sqrt{57}$ is bigger than 3. ($\sqrt{9} = 3$)

31) Choice A is correct

Volume of a right cylinder $= \pi r^2 h \rightarrow 50\pi = \pi r^2 h = \pi (2)^2 h \rightarrow h = 12.5$, The height of the cylinder is 12.5 inches which is bigger than 10 inches.

32) Choice A is correct.

Simplify quantity B. Quantity B: $(\frac{x}{6})^6 = \frac{x^6}{6^6}$, Since, the two quantities have the same numerator (x^6) and the denominator in quantity B is bigger ($6^6 > 6$), then the quantity A is greater. (remember that x is an integer)

33) Choice D is correct.

Choose different values for x and find the value of quantity A. $x = 1$, then:

Quantity A: $\frac{1}{x} + x = \frac{1}{1} + 1 = 2$,

Quantity B is greater, $x = 0.1$, then:

Quantity A: $\frac{1}{x} + x = \frac{1}{0.1} + 1 = 10 + 1 = 11$,

Quantity A is greater. The relationship cannot be determined from the information given.

34) Choice D is correct

Simply change the fractions to decimals. $\frac{4}{5} = 0.80$, $\frac{6}{7} = 0.857\ldots$, $\frac{5}{6} = 0.8333\ldots$,

As you can see, x lies between 0.80 and 0.857... and it can be 0.81 or 0.84. The first one is less than 0.833... and the second one is greater than 0.833... . The relationship cannot be determined from the information given.

35) Choice C is correct

Choose different values for a and b and find the values of quantity A and quantity B.

$a = 2$ and $b = 3$, then: Quantity A: $|2 - 3| = |-1| = 1$, Quantity B: $|3 - 2| = |1| = 1$

The two quantities are equal. $a = -3$ and $b = 2$, then:

Quantity A: $|-3 - 2| = |-5| = 5$, Quantity B: $|2 - (-3)| = |2 + 3| = 5$

The two quantities are equal. Any other values of a and b give the same answer.

36) Choice A is correct

$2x^3 + 10 = 64 \rightarrow 2x^3 = 64 - 10 = 54 \rightarrow x^3 = \frac{54}{2} = 27 \rightarrow x = \sqrt[3]{27} = \sqrt[3]{3^3} = 3$

$120 - 18y = 84 \rightarrow -18y = 84 - 120 = -36 \rightarrow y = \frac{-36}{-18} = 2$

37) Choice C is correct.

Quantity A is: $\frac{3+4+x}{3} = 3 \rightarrow x = 2$, Quantity B is: $\frac{2+(2-6)+(2+4)+(2\times2)}{4} = 2$

ISEE Middle LEVEL Math Practice Test 1 Section 2

1) Choice C is correct

50% of 46 is: $\frac{50}{100} \times 46 = \frac{46}{2} = 23$, Let x be the number then: $x = 23 - 5 = 18$

2) Choice C is correct

$4 \times \left(\frac{1}{3} - \frac{1}{6}\right) + 5 = 4 \times \left(\frac{2-1}{6}\right) + 5 = \frac{4}{6} + 5 = \frac{2}{3} + 5 = \frac{17}{3} = 5.6 \dots$

3) Choice A is correct

20% of $120 = \frac{20}{100} \times 120 = 24$, Let x be the number, then, $x = 24 + 15 = 39$

4) Choice D is correct

Number of pencils are blue$= 85 - 42 = 43$, Percent of blue pencils is:

$\frac{43}{85} \times 100 = 50.58\% \approx 51\%$

5) Choice D is correct

$(x + 6)^3 = 64 \rightarrow x + 6 = \sqrt[3]{64} \rightarrow \sqrt[3]{4^3} = 4 \rightarrow x + 6 = 4 \rightarrow x = 4 - 6 = -2$

6) Choice B is correct

The ratio of red to blue balls is $3 : 2$. Then: $\frac{3}{2} = \frac{x}{90} \rightarrow x = \frac{90 \times 3}{2} = 135$

7) Choice C is correct

The perimeter of rectangle is: $2 \times (5 + 8) = 2 \times 13 = 26$

The perimeter of circle is: $2\pi r = 2 \times 3 \times \frac{12}{2} = 36$,

Difference in perimeter is: $36 - 26 = 10$

8) Choice C is correct

Let x be the number. Write the equation and solve for x. $(27 - x) \div x = 2$, Multiply both sides by x. $(28 - x) = 2x$, then add x both sides. $27 = 3x$, now divide both sides by 3. $x = 9$

9) Choice A is correct

If $\frac{3x}{2} = 15$, then $3x = 30 \rightarrow x = 10$, $\frac{2x}{5} = \frac{2 \times 10}{5} = \frac{20}{5} = 4$

10) Choice B is correct

Use this formula: Percent of Change $= \frac{New\ Value - Old\ Value}{Old\ Value} \times 100\%$

$\frac{15,000 - 20,000}{20,000} \times 100\% = -25\%$ (negative signs means the price decreased)

11) Choice C is correct

$\frac{1}{4} = 0.25$; $\frac{7}{9} = 0.77$; $75\% = 0.75$

0.85 is the greatest number provided.

12) Choice D is correct

$Area = \pi r^2 = \pi \times (\frac{10}{2})^2 = 25\pi = 25 \times 3.14 = 78.5$

13) Choice C is correct

Only choice C is equal to 90.

$\left(\left(\frac{3}{2} + 3\right) \times \frac{18}{3}\right) + 63 = \left(\left(\frac{3+6}{2}\right) \times \frac{18}{3}\right) + 63 = \left(\frac{9}{2} \times \frac{18}{3}\right) + 63 = 27 + 63 = 90$

14) Choice A is correct

All angles in a triangle sum up to 180 degrees. Then:

$2\alpha + 90° = 180° \rightarrow 2\alpha = 90 \rightarrow \alpha = 45°$

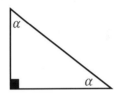

15) Choice B is correct

First, find the number. Let x be the number. Write the equation and solve for x.

120% of a number is 84, then: $1.2 \times x = 84 \Rightarrow x = 84 \div 1.2 = 70$

90% of 70 is: $0.9 \times 70 = 63$

16) Choice D is correct

Find the difference of each pairs of numbers: $3, 4, 6, 9, 13, 18, 24, \_\_, 39$

The difference of 3 and 4 is 1, 4 and 6 is 2, 6 and 9 is 3, 9 and 13 is 4, 13 and 18 is 5, 18 and 24 is 6, 24 and next number should be 7. The number is $24 + 7 = 31$

17) Choice B is correct

The sum of angles in rectangle is $360°$

18) Choice A is correct

Let x be the number of shoes the team can purchase. Therefore, the team can purchase $130x$.

The team had $25,000 and spent $15,000. Now the team can spend on new shoes $10,000 at most. Now, write the inequality: $130x + 15,000 \leq 25,000$

19) Choice C is correct

The capacity of a red box is 30% greater than a blue box. Let x be the capacity of the blue box. Then: $x + 30\%\ of\ x = 52 \rightarrow 1.3x = 52 \rightarrow x = \frac{52}{1.3} = 40$

20) Choice B is correct

$\frac{1.75}{1.40} = 1.25 = 125\%$

21) Choice C is correct

$\frac{2}{3} \times 30 = \frac{60}{3} = 20$

22) Choice B is correct

$60 \ minutes \ = 1 \ Hours \rightarrow \frac{190}{60} = 3.16 \ Hours$

23) Choice D is correct

58 is not prime number, it is divisible by 2 and 29.

24) Choice C is correct

The area of the square is 36 inches. Therefore, the side of the square is square root of the area. $\sqrt{36} = 6$ inches, four times the side of the square is the perimeter:

$4 \times 6 = 24$ inches

25) Choice D is correct

$13 is what percent of $26? $13 \div 26 = 0.50 = 50\%$

26) Choice D is correct

$\$1.80 \div 36 = \$0.05$

27) Choice A is correct

Let x be one-kilogram orange cost, then: $2x + (2 \times 4.2) = 26.4 \rightarrow 2x + 8.4 = 26.4 \rightarrow 2x = 26.4 - 8.4 \rightarrow 2x = 18 \rightarrow x = \frac{18}{2} = \$9$

28) Choice D is correct

Use PEMDAS (order of operation):

$[6 \times (-24) + 8] - (-4) + [6 \times 5] \div 2 = [-144 \ + \ 8] - (-4) + [30] \div 2 = [-144 \ + \ 8] - (-4) + 15 = [-136] - (-4) + 15 = [-136] + 4 + 15 = -117$

29) Choice B is correct

The width of a rectangle is $3x$ and its length is $5x$. Therefore, the perimeter of the rectangle is $16x$. $Perimeter \ of \ a \ rectangle = 2(width + length) = 2(3x + 5x) = 2(8x) = 16x$

The perimeter of the rectangle is 80. Then: $16x = 80 \rightarrow x = 5$

30)Choice D is correct

The distance between Jason and Joe is 15 miles. Jason running at 5.5 miles per hour and Joe is running at the speed of 7 miles per hour. Therefore, every hour the distance is 1.5 miles less. $15 \div 1.5 = 10$

31)Choice D is correct

$$\Big(\big((-12) + 20\big) \times 3\Big) + (-16) = \big((8) \times 3\big) - 16 = 24 - 16 = 8$$

32)Choice A is correct

The percent of girls playing tennis is: $45\% \times 20\% = 0.45 \times 0.20 = 0.09 = 9\%$

33)Choice D is correct

Let x be the original price. If the price of the sofa is decreased by 30% to $490, then: $70\% \ of \ x = 490 \Rightarrow 0.70x = 490 \Rightarrow x = 490 \div 0.70 = 700$

34)Choice A is correct

There are twice as many boys as girls. Let x be the number of girls in the class. Then: $x + 2x = 45 \rightarrow 3x = 45 \rightarrow x = 15$

35)Choice C is correct

The ratio of lions to tigers is 5 to 3 at the zoo. Therefore, total number of lions and tigers must be divisible by 8. $5 + 3 = 8$, From the numbers provided, only 97 is not divisible by 8.

36)Choice A is correct

$$10x = -55.5 + 15.5 = -40 \rightarrow x = \frac{-40}{10} = -4$$

37)Choice A is correct

0.25 minutes equals 15 seconds. Then, the number of rotates in 15 second= $\frac{400 \times 15}{5} = 1,200$

38)Choice A is correct

Use formula of rectangle prism volume. $V = (length)(width)(height) \Rightarrow$

$2,500 = (40) (10) (height) \Rightarrow height = 2,500 \div 400 = 6.25$

39)Choice C is correct

$7,776 = 6^5 \rightarrow 6^x = 6^5 \rightarrow x = 5$

40) Choice B is correct

$10 + 5(x + 5 - 5x) = 10 + 5(-4x + 5) = 40 \rightarrow 10 - 20x + 25 = 40 \rightarrow -20x + 35 = 40 \rightarrow -20x = 5 \rightarrow x = -\frac{1}{4}$

41) Choice B is correct

The area of trapezoid is: $\left(\frac{8+10}{2}\right) \times 5 = 45$

42) Choice D is correct

$13.125 \div 0.005 = \dfrac{\frac{13,125}{1,000}}{\frac{5}{1,000}} = \dfrac{13,125}{5} = 2,625$

43) Choice B is correct

The probability of choosing a Hearts is $\frac{13}{52} = \frac{1}{4}$

44) Choice B is correct

$20 - 13.59 = \$6.41$

45) Choice C is correct

$\dfrac{5 \times 20}{80} = \dfrac{100}{80} = 1.25 \approx 1.3$

46) Choice C is correct

Write the equation and solve for B: $0.60A = 0.30B$, divide both sides by 0.30, then you will have $\frac{0.60}{0.30}A = B$, therefore: $B = 2A$, and B is 2 times of A or it's 200% of A.

47) Choice C is correct

$\dfrac{3}{4} + \dfrac{\frac{-3}{5}}{\frac{6}{10}} = \dfrac{3}{4} + \dfrac{(-3) \times 10}{5 \times 6} = \dfrac{3}{4} + \dfrac{-30}{30} = \dfrac{3}{4} - 1 = \dfrac{3-4}{4} = -\dfrac{1}{4}$

ISEE Middle LEVEL Math Practice Test 2 Section 1

1) Choice A is correct

$343 = 7^3 \rightarrow \dfrac{7^x}{7} = 7^3 \rightarrow 7^{x-1} = 7^3 \rightarrow x - 1 = 3 \rightarrow x = 4$

2) Choice B is correct

In triangle sum of all angles equal to 180° then:

$y = 180° - (120° + 30°) = 180° - 150° = 30°$

3) Choice B is correct

$\dfrac{1}{3} \approx 0.33; \dfrac{4}{7} \approx 0.57; \dfrac{8}{12} \approx 0.66; \dfrac{3}{4} = 0.75$

4) Choice C is correct

One hour equal to 60 minutes then, $5 \, hours = 5 \times 60 = 300 \, minutes$

One minute equal to 60 seconds then, $300 \, minutes = 300 \times 60 = 18,000 \, seconds$

Distance that travel by object is: $0.4 \times 18,000 = 7,200 \, cm = 72 \, m$

5) Choice B is correct

Number of visiting fans: $\dfrac{2 \times 24,000}{5} = 9,600$

6) Choice A is correct

Circumference of circle$= 2\pi r = 2\pi \times \dfrac{17}{2} = 17\pi \sim 53.38 \, m$

7) Choice B is correct

The lowest common multiple of 24 and 36 is 72.

8) Choice A is correct

Area of circle with diameter 8 is: $\pi r^2 = \pi \left(\dfrac{8}{2}\right)^2 = 16\pi$, The area of shaded region is: $\dfrac{16\pi}{4} = 4\pi$

9) Choice D is correct

30% of $200 = \dfrac{30}{100} \times 200 = 60$, Final sale price is: $200 - 60 = \$140$

10) Choice D is correct

To find the discount, multiply the number by $(100\% - rate \ of \ discount)$.

Therefore, for the first discount we get: $(300)(100\% - 15\%) = (300)(0.85)$

For the next 25% discount: $(300)(0.85)(0.75)$

11) Choice C is correct

The amount of petrol consumed after x hours is: $5x$, Petrol remaining: $70 - 5x$

12) Choice A is correct

$4 + x + 8\left(\frac{x}{4}\right) = 2x + 12 \to 4 + x + 2x = 2x + 12 \to x = 8$

13) Choice B is correct

The area of trapezoid is: $\left(\frac{16+18}{2}\right)x = 136 \to 17x = 136 \to x = 8$

14) Choice A is correct

$\frac{3}{5}$ of $280 = \frac{3}{5} \times 280 = 168$, $\frac{1}{2}$ of $168 = \frac{1}{2} \times 168 = 84$, $\frac{1}{3}$ of $84 = \frac{1}{3} \times 84 = 28$

15) Choice B is correct

$6 + 3x \le 21 \to 3x \le 21 - 6 \to 3x \le 15 \to x \le \frac{15}{3} \to x \le 5$,   Then: $a = 5$

16) Choice B is correct

One liter $= 1,000\ cm^3 \to 7\ liters = 7,000\ cm^3$, $7,000 = 25 \times 5 \times h \to h = \frac{7,000}{125} = 56\ cm$

17) Choice C is correct

$4f + 4g = 4x - 2y \to 4f + 4(2y - 6x) = 4x - 2y \to 4f + 8y - 24x = 4x - 2y \to$

$4f = 28x - 10y \to 2f = 14x - 5y$

18) Choice A is correct

$\frac{\frac{13}{3} \times \frac{4}{5}}{\frac{10}{30}} = -\frac{\frac{13 \times 4}{3 \times 5}}{\frac{10}{30}} = -\frac{\frac{52}{15}}{\frac{10}{30}} = -\frac{52 \times 30}{15 \times 10} = -10.4$

19) Choice A is correct

Use Pythagorean theorem to find the value of c:

$a^2 + b^2 = c^2 \to 5^2 + 12^2 = c^2 \to 169 = c^2 \to c = 13$.

Perimeter of parallelogram$= (9 + 5 + 13) \times 2 = 54$

20) Choice C is correct

$\frac{6}{50} \times 100 = \frac{6}{5} \times 10 = 12\%$

21) Choice A is correct

Let x be the integer. Then: $2x - 3 = 71$, Add 3 both sides: $2x = 74$, Divide both sides by 2: $x = 37$

22) Choice D is correct

$$\frac{0.35}{8.5} \times 100 = 4.11 \approx 4.00$$

23) Choice D is correct

Plug in 140 for F and then solve for C. $C = \frac{5}{9}(F - 32) \Rightarrow C = \frac{5}{9}(140 - 32) \Rightarrow$

$$C = \frac{5}{9}(108) = 60$$

24) Choice D is correct

$$Average = \frac{sum\ of\ terms}{number\ of\ terms} \Rightarrow 20 = \frac{14+16+21+x}{4} \Rightarrow 80 = 51 + x \Rightarrow x = 29$$

25) Choice B is correct

First write the numbers in the order: 2,2,2,3,3,4,4,5,5,6,6

The mode of numbers is: 2; median is: 4

26) Choice A is correct.

Column A: Simplify. $\frac{\sqrt{64-48}}{\sqrt{25-9}} = \frac{\sqrt{16}}{\sqrt{16}} = 1$

Column B: $\frac{(7-4)}{(8-3)} = \frac{3}{5}$

27) Choice B is correct

$2x^5 - 9 = 477 \rightarrow 2x^5 = 477 + 9 = 486 \rightarrow x^5 = \frac{486}{2} = 243 \rightarrow x = \sqrt[5]{243} = \sqrt[5]{3^5} = 3$

$\frac{1}{3} - \frac{y}{5} = -\frac{7}{15} \rightarrow \frac{y}{5} = \frac{1}{3} + \frac{7}{15} = \frac{5+7}{15} = \frac{12}{15} = \frac{4}{5} \rightarrow y = 5 \times \frac{4}{5} = 4$

28) Choice A is correct.

Column A: First, find the integers. Let x be the smallest integer. Then the integers are x, $(x + 1)$, and $(x + 2)$. The sum of the integers is -45. Then:

$$x + x + 1 + x + 2 = -45 \rightarrow 3x + 3 = -45 \rightarrow 3x = -48 \rightarrow x = -16$$

The smallest integer is -16, therefore, the largest integer is bigger than that.

29) Choice C is correct.

Column A: $4^2 - 2^4 = 16 - 16 = 0$

Column B: $2^4 - 4^2 = 16 - 16 = 0$

30)Choice C is correct.

Column A: 8% of the computer cost is 20: $8\% \times 250 = 0.08 \times 250 = 20$

Column B: 20

31)Choice C is correct.

Column A: The slope of the line $4x + 2y = 7$ is -2.

Write the equation in slope intercept form. $4x + 2y = 7 \rightarrow 2y = -4x + 7 \rightarrow y = -2x + \frac{7}{2}$

Column B: The slope of the line that passes through points $(2, 5)$ and $(3, 3)$:

Use slope formula: $slope \ of \ a \ line = \frac{y_2 - y_1}{x_2 - x_1} = \frac{3-5}{3-2} = -2$

32)Choice A is correct

prime factoring of 55 is: 5×11 , prime factoring of 210 is: $2 \times 3 \times 5 \times 7$

Quantity $A = 5$ and Quantity $B = 2$

33)Choice A is correct.

Column A: Simplify. $\sqrt{144 - 81} = \sqrt{63}$

Column B: $\sqrt{144} - \sqrt{81} = 12 - 9 = 3$

$\sqrt{63}$ is bigger than 3. ($\sqrt{9} = 3$)

34)Choice B is correct

6% of $x = 5\%$ of $y \rightarrow 0.06 \, x = 0.05 \, y \rightarrow x = \frac{0.05}{0.06}y \rightarrow x = \frac{5}{6}y$, therefore, y is bigger than x.

35)Choice C is correct

Simplify both quantities.

Quantity A: $(-5)^4 = (-5) \times (-5) \times (-5) \times (-5) = 625$

Quantity B: $5 \times 5 \times 5 \times 5 = 625$

The two quantities are equal.

36)Choice C is correct.

Use exponent "product rule": $x^n \times x^m = x^{n+m}$

Quantity A: $(1.88)^4(1.88)^8 = (1.88)^{4+8} = (1.88)^{12}$

Quantity B: $(1.88)^{12}$

The two quantities are equal.

37) Choice D is correct.

Choose different values for x and find the value of quantity A and quantity B.

$x = 1$, then: Quantity A: $x^{10} = 1^{10} = 1$

Quantity B: $x^{20} = 1^{20} = 1$

The two quantities are equal.

$x = 2$, then: Quantity A: $x^{10} = 2^{10}$

Quantity B: $x^{20} = 2^{20}$

Quantity B is greater.

Therefore, the relationship cannot be determined from the information given

ISEE Middle LEVEL Math Practice Test 2 Section 2

1) Choice A is correct

20 cubed is: $20^3 = 8,000$

2) Choice A is correct

$3^x + 28 = 55 \rightarrow 3^x = 55 - 28 = 27$ and $27 = 3^3$, $3^x = 3^3 \rightarrow x = 3$

3) Choice D is correct

All angles in a parallelogram sum up to 360 degrees. Since, we only have 2 angles, therefore the answer cannot be determined.

4) Choice D is correct

Prime factorizing of $10 = 2 \times 5$, Prime factorizing of $35 = 5 \times 7$

$x = LCM = 2 \times 5 \times 7 = 70$, $\frac{70}{5} + 2 = 14 + 2 = 16$

5) Choice B is correct

The area of trapezoid is: $\left(\frac{8+12}{2}\right) \times x = 30 \rightarrow 10x = 30 \rightarrow x = 3$

$y = \sqrt{3^2 + 4^2} = 5$, Perimeter is: $12 + 3 + 8 + 5 = 28$

6) Choice B is correct

Swing moves once from point A to point B and returns to point A is: $20 + 20 = 40$ seconds

Therefore, for ten times: $5 \times 40 = 200$ seconds

7) Choice D is correct

Speed of the blue car: $1\frac{2}{5} \times 40 = 56$, Difference of the cars' speed: $56 - 40 = 16$, The red car is $12\ km$ ahead of a blue car. Therefore, it takes the blue car 45 minutes to catch the red car. $\frac{12}{16} = \frac{3}{3}$ Hour = 45 minutes

8) Choice D is correct

The population is increased by 10% and 25%. 10% increase changes the population to 110% of original population. For the second increase, multiply the result by 125%.

$(1.10) \times (1.25) = 1.37 = 137\%$, 37 percent of the population is increased after two years.

9) Choice C is correct

Use PEMDAS (order of operation): $5 + 8 \times (-2) - [4 + 22 \times 5] \div 6 = 5 + 8 \times (-2) - [4 + 110] \div 6 = 5 + 8 \times (-2) - [114] \div 6 = 5 + (-16) - 19 = 5 + (-16) - 19 = -11 - 19 = -30$

10) Choice A is correct

Let x be the number of years. Therefore, $2,500 per year equals $2,500x$. starting from $26,000 annual salary means you should add that amount to $2,500x$. Income more than that is: $I > 2,500\,x + 26,000$

11) Choice D is correct

Angle between $90°$ and $180°$ is called obtuse angle.

12) Choice A is correct

2,500 out of 65,000 equals to $\frac{2,500}{65,000} = \frac{25}{650} = \frac{1}{26}$

13) Choice B is correct

$Probability = \frac{number\ of\ desired\ outcomes}{number\ of\ total\ outcomes} = \frac{19}{13+19+19+25} = \frac{19}{76} = \frac{1}{4}$

14) Choice D is correct

Only choice D equals 110: $(2 \times 10) + (50 \times 1.5) + 15 = 20 + 75 + 15 = 110$

15) Choice D is correct

The area of rectangle is: $8 \times 4 = 32\ cm^2$,The area of circle is:

$\pi r^2 = \pi \times (\frac{8}{2})^2 = 3 \times 16 = 48$, Difference in area is: $48 - 32 = 16$

16) Choice B is correct

$x^2 + 2x + 1 = (x + 1)^2 \rightarrow (x + 1)^2 = 64 \rightarrow x + 1 = 8 \rightarrow x = 7\ or\ x + 1 = -8 \rightarrow$

$x = -9$

17) Choice C is correct

Perimeter $A = 4 \times 6 = 24$, Area $B = 2 \times 4 = 8$, $\frac{24}{8} = 3$

18) Choice A is correct

$\frac{18 \times 21}{5} = \frac{378}{5} = 75.6$

19) Choice B is correct

To find the number of possible outfit combinations, multiply number of options for each factor: $4 \times 2 \times 5 = 40$

20) Choice A is correct

Let x be the number, then: $x^2 + 9 = 25 \rightarrow x^2 = 16 \rightarrow x^2 - 16 = 0 \rightarrow (x + 4)(x - 4) = 0 \rightarrow x = 4 \ or \ x = -4$

21) Choice D is correct

8% of \$2,000 $= \frac{8}{100} \times 2,000 = \$160$

22) Choice A is correct

$\frac{x}{4} + \frac{5}{4} = \frac{30}{6} \rightarrow \frac{x}{4} = 5 - \frac{5}{4} = \frac{20 - 5}{4} = \frac{15}{4} = \frac{x}{4} \rightarrow x = 4 \times \frac{15}{4} = 15$

23) Choice D is correct

$y = 5ab + 3b^3$, Plug in the values of a and b in the equation: $a = 3$ and $b = 2$

$y = 5\,(3)(2) + 3\,(2)^3 = 30 + 3(8) = 30 + 24 = 54$

24) Choice D is correct

$|6 - 10| = |-4| = 4$

25) Choice C is correct

The angles of an equilateral triangle are $60, 60, 60$ degrees.

26) Choice C is correct

$9x - 10 = 5\left(\frac{4}{5}x - y\right) + 5 \rightarrow 9x - 10 = 4x - 5y + 5 \rightarrow 5x - 10 = -5y + 5$

$\rightarrow 5x = -5y + 15 \rightarrow x = -y + 3 \rightarrow x + y = 3$

27) Choice C is correct

The area of the floor is: $7cm \times 27\ cm = 189\ cm^2$, The number is tiles needed $= 189 \div 3 = 63$

28) Choice B is correct

Let x be price of one-kilogram of apple and y be price of one-kilogram of orange, then:

$x = 2y, 2x + 3y = 21 \rightarrow 2(2y) + 3y = 21 \rightarrow 7y = 21 \rightarrow y = \frac{21}{7} = 3 \rightarrow x = 2 \times 3 = 6$

29) Choice D is correct

122 is not prime number, it is divided by 2

30) Choice D is correct

Since, each of the x students in a team may invite up to 6 friends, the maximum number of people in the party is 7 times x or $7x$. (*one student + 6 friends = 7 people*)

31) Choice C is correct

Perimeter $= 2\pi r = 2 \times \pi \times \frac{10}{2} = 10\pi \approx 31.4 \approx 31$

32) Choice B is correct

$60 \ minutes = 1 \ Hour \rightarrow \frac{280}{60} = 4.6 \ Hours$

33) Choice A is correct

Let x be the weight of the red box. Then: Weight of blue box: $0.8x = 60 \rightarrow x = \frac{60}{0.8} = 75$,

Weight of yellow box $1.20y = 75 \rightarrow y = 62.5$

The weight of all boxes: $60 + 75 + 62.5 = 197.5$

34) Choice D is correct

$180° - 40° = 140°$

35) Choice B is correct

Average speed: $\frac{350}{9} = 38.8 \ miles \ per \ hour$

36) Choice B is correct

Let x be the price that third person has to pay then; $58 = 7.5 + (2 \times 7.5) + x \rightarrow$

$x = 58 - 22.5 = 35.5$

37) Choice D is correct

$\left(\left((-15) + 40\right) \times \frac{1}{5}\right) + (-15) = \left((25) \times \frac{1}{5}\right) - 15 = 5 - 15 = -10$

38) Choice D is correct

$138,210 = 1.3821 \times 10^5$

39) Choice B is correct

$(10 - 6)! = 4! = 4 \times 3 \times 2 \times 1 = 24$

40) Choice D is correct

$c = \sqrt{4^2 + 3^2} = \sqrt{25} = 5$, Perimeter is: $5 + 3 + 4 = 12$

41) Choice A is correct

Let x be the number then, 150% of $= 1.5x$, $1.5x = 0.30 \times 80 = 24 \rightarrow x = \frac{24}{1.5} = 16$

42) Choice A is correct

Number of employees with Diploma: $\frac{4 \times 24}{1} = 96$

That means there are 24 employees with bachelor's degree and 96 employees with high school diploma. To get the ratio of employees with bachelor's degree to the number of employees with High School Diploma 3 to 4, there should be 32 employees with high school diploma. So, 40 ($96 - 32 = 64$) employees with High School Diploma should be moved to other departments.

43) Choice B is correct

Use Pythagorean theorem: $x^2 + 20^2 = 25^2 \rightarrow x^2 = 25^2 - 20^2 \rightarrow x = \sqrt{25^2 - 20^2} \rightarrow x = \sqrt{625 - 400} = \sqrt{225} = 15$

44) Choice D is correct

$average = \frac{sum\ of\ terms}{number\ of\ terms}$, The sum of the weight of all girls is: $20 \times 65 = 1,300\ kg$

The sum of the weight of all boys is: $35 \times 72 = 2,520\ kg$, The sum of the weight of all students is: $1,300 + 2,520 = 3,820\ kg$, $Average = \frac{3,820}{55} = 69.45$

45) Choice A is correct

The sum of supplement angles is 180. Let x be that angle. Therefore, $x + 9x = 180$, $10x = 180$, divide both sides by 10: $x = 18$

46) Choice D is correct

Smallest 5–digit number is 10,000, and biggest 5–digit number is 99,999. The difference is: 89,999 ,

47) Choice A is correct

The average speed of john is: $140 \div 5 = 28$, The average speed of Alice is: $210 \div 3 = 70$

Write the ratio and simplify. $28 : 70 \Rightarrow 2 : 5$

Receive the PDF version of this book or get another FREE book!

Thank you for using our Book!

Do you LOVE this book?

Then, you can get the PDF version of this book or another book absolutely FREE!

Please email us at:

info@EffortlessMath.com

for details.

Author's Final Note

I hope you enjoyed reading this book. You've made it through the book! Great job!

First of all, thank you for purchasing this study guide. I know you could have picked any number of books to help you prepare for your ISEE Middle Level test, but you picked this book and for that I am extremely grateful.

It took me years to write this prep book for the ISEE Middle Level because I wanted to prepare a comprehensive ISEE Middle Level book to help test takers make the most effective use of their valuable time while preparing for the test.

After teaching and tutoring math courses for over a decade, I've gathered my personal notes and lessons to develop this study guide. It is my greatest hope that the lessons in this book could help you prepare for your test successfully.

If you have any questions, please contact me at reza@effortlessmath.com and I will be glad to assist. Your feedback will help me to greatly improve the quality of my books in the future and make this book even better. Furthermore, I expect that I have made a few minor errors somewhere in this book. If you think this to be the case, please let me know so I can fix the issue as soon as possible.

If you enjoyed this book and found some benefit in reading this, I'd like to hear from you and hope that you could take a quick minute to post a review on the book's Amazon page. To leave your valuable feedback, please visit: amzn.to/3pcpCvY

Or scan this QR code.

I personally go over every single review, to make sure my books really are reaching out and helping students and test takers. Please help me help ISEE test takers, by leaving a review!

I wish you all the best in your future success!

Reza Nazari

Math teacher and author

55328894R00107